Finally Meeting Mum

Mike Daligan

Edale Press London

Published by Edale Press in 2021

ISBN 978-1-9998764-1-8

Cover Design by Paul Flowers with
additional suggestions by Gaynor Daligan

Typesetting by Divya Venkatesh

By the same author:
The Real Big Society and My Part In It
The Other Side Of The Doors
Lessons from a Chequered Life
'Why Don't You Just Support Arsenal?'

www.mikedaligan.com

Edale Press London

Contents

The Child

Wake up with eyes still shut.
Don't open. Not yet.
Keep shut. Stay dark. Stay warm.
Warm dark is safe. Awake time is bad.
Voices downstairs.
Get up time.
No, not yet. Keep OK time.
Is she alright?
Why she not here?
Where is she?
Be with him. Hold him.
Eyes open.
Auntie Doll.
Michael. It's time to get up.
No! Daytime was bad time. Sick time. Worry time.
Night was better time. Eyes close time. Not scary time.
Be 'how it was' time.
She here. She OK. She mum.
Soon be in heaven. Where is heaven?
Nice place.
Can he be in nice place too?
Don't know.

Michael, up you get. Breakfast is ready.

Open eyes. Feet out. Cold.

Cold outside warmer than cold inside.

Don't feel. Feel hurts.

Hands help him. Clothes on. Downstairs. Cold water on face. Towel.

Into kitchen. Fire there. Warm outside but still cold inside.

Michael, eat your porridge. Don't let it get cold. It's got treacle on it.

Spoon in mouth. Sweet, sticky, warm. Inside warm but only tummy. Other places hurt.

When did hurt begin?

Finish porridge.

Michael, if you're going out, not too far and put your coat on.

He opened the front door.

Cold outside meets cold inside him.

Voices whisper in the street.

Poor little mite.

Mind your own business.

Anyway he's not a mite, he's little man.

How's she been, Doll?

Going downhill fast.

He's asked for a bloody divorce. It seems there's someone else.

Again? How many times is that?

I just wish I could get her to live again.

Fat chance of that. Dropsy doesn't get better, you know and now there's some bloody kidney problem.

Yes I know. His letter seems like the final straw. When she read it, she gave up. All she ever thought of was Michael and being with that bastard so that they could be a family again.

Like I said, fat chance. What did the doctor say?

If she goes on like this, not eating or drinking properly on top of the weak heart, not long.

Days, weeks?

Even if it's weeks, not many of them.

What about Michael?

Bob and me will take care of him.

He's like Bob's own and you know that we'll do whatever we can.

Does she know what's happening?

Yes, she does but I don't think that she's got any fight left.

Poor cow.

She's exhausted and frightened for the child.

Where is he?

Playing.

Not at school?

She wants him near. It helps her. And it's just in case.

The door flies open.

There you are, Michael.

Where's mummy?

She's in bed asleep. You can go up but not too much noise.

I'll be quiet. Just cuddle her.

She'll like that from her little man.

Smiley face and good inside. He'll always look after her.

Somehow he knew that always wasn't a long time.

Uncle Bob called him. He knew it wasn't good.

Michael, you need to be brave. Mummy needs you to be strong for her. You love mummy, don't you?

Yes, silly. She's mine. Not for anyone else. Just me.

Yes she is but she's just waking up so go and tell her that you'll be good. For her.

Of course I will.

She had pillows round her to keep her up and her eyes kept closing.

Just sit next to her, Michael, and give her a kiss.

I always kiss her.

A special one this time and hold her hand to let her know you're there.

He didn't need to be told that, thank you.

Hello, Mummy. It's me.

Her eyes opened. Just.

Hello, Michael. She reached out to hold him. I love you, little man.

She looked very tired and very, very sad.

Don't worry, Mummy. I'm here.

Grow up big and strong for me.

I will be big and strong when I grow up.

Is your father here yet?

Her voice was very quiet and there was a smell like he'd pee'd his trousers.

No. Is daddy coming to stay with us?

She was crying as she held him.

Don't worry, Mummy. We'll be alright.

Her eyes closed again.

Mummy, wake up I want to talk to you.

He saw her eyes open again. Even more tired and sad than before.

He saw her lips move but couldn't hear any words.

Mummy, wake up.

Uncle Bob picked him up. Come on, soldier, let's you and me make a cup of tea.

When he went to bed that night, there were still people around and he felt frightened.

Why couldn't he sleep with mummy as he always did?

She needs lots of sleep, Michael, and you might disturb her.

I wouldn't do that. I'd just cuddle her and make sure that she's alright.

She's mummy. She needs me.

Another sleep and lots of people in the house.

Then the door opened again. It was Uncle Lal with a man in a soldier's uniform.

Hello, my boy. Sorry I took so long to get here but I had a long journey.

It was his father.

He felt himself lifted up and hugged.

Don't worry, it'll all be alright. Now let's go and see your mum.

Lal led the way but why were they all looking away as his father walked by?

That poor child. What will happen to him?

Shush, he'll hear you.

And he did, but why was he poor?

When they got into the bedroom, Uncle Bob took no notice

of his father.

Bob, she's asked for Michael,

Bob led him forward.

Up you get, Michael.

Give your mum a kiss and tell her how much you love her.

But she's asleep.

It's OK. Lou, he's here.

She opened her eyes. Sunken and dark rimmed, wet with tears and sad beyond measure.

He saw her mouth move but couldn't hear what she said.

Put your ear as close as you can, Michael.

It was Uncle Bob.

Hello, my little man.

Then he heard her breathe deeply.

Promise me that you'll always be a good boy.

I am a good boy, Mummy.

Grow big and strong for me.

He smiled.

Of course I will.

Again, she breathed very deeply.

He thought he heard her say "love".

Then she closed her eyes again.

He turned to look at his father.

Daddy, come here but his father stayed where he was.

He heard Uncle Bob say that they should go downstairs.

He'd give him a push on the swing.

They hadn't been there long when Auntie Doll came out to join them. She was crying. Lots.

Uncle Bob went over and put his arms around his sister.

She's gone Bob.

They both looked at him and reached over to hold him. Very, very tightly.

After some minutes, still together, they walked back into the house.

A Very Bad Thing Happened

Something very bad had happened. So bad, in fact, that nothing could be worse. He'd known that something was going to happen. A letter had arrived from "your father". Already very ill, it pushed his mother over the edge. Still with his unit in Germany after the war, he'd met someone else and wanted a divorce. Whatever that was, it meant that he wouldn't be coming home. Ever! It also meant that they wouldn't have any money coming in. They would be "on the street" and he would be taken away from her. All this against a background of sickness, despair and anger. It was then that, when he met her again over twenty years later, Aunt Doll his mum's sister, told him that his mum had given up caring for herself, not even bothering to wash or comb her hair, and that he was left to "run wild". Fortunately his Uncle Bob and Doll took over but they weren't her. After a few weeks, she didn't get out of bed any more.

Finally, he was taken upstairs to her bedroom. It was full of adults crying. She held him tightly and told him that she loved him and that he must be a good boy. Then she was gone. But where to? Uncle Bob took him into the garden that night to show him the stars and to tell him that his mum was now one of them. He knew that wasn't true. She was in the front room. Only used on special occasions, it was where he was taken to "say goodbye". The room smelt of flowers and his mum was asleep in a shiny wooden box. "Say goodbye to mummy, Michael" was all he remembered. Yet for many years afterwards he had nightmares about the 'whale's teeth' which he later discovered to be an image of the curtain like gathers in the material around the edge of the coffin. That image petrified him for much of his life. The following day, while the rest of the country was celebrating the wedding of the future queen, Alice Hudson, a widow these past 15 years, was mourning the death of another daughter. At the same age and as a result of a similar childhood illness to the first. All the while trying to care for the elder daughter's children and another small child who was distraught at the absence of his mother. Along with his persistent queries as to when his father would be coming to see them again. In this latter request, he didn't have to wait that long as his father did just that the following day to take him out. They were going to see his "Auntie Ada". Holding his father's hand, they walked along Silwood Street, where the old engine was parked on the railway tracks high above them, and along to Galleywall Road before they turned into Lynton Road. As they walked, his father talked of a big adventure that he would soon be taking. He doesn't remember very much of the visit to his aunt's, although he later found out that the words 'boys' home' were mentioned. They then returned home and his father left him with Aunt Doll as he "had some things to do". As he left, he heard her say, "Dorrie, we need to talk about what's going to happen." It was soon after that the child realised that the 'big adventure' was something that he would undertake on his own. He also discovered that journeys were always better than destinations.

That night, Aunt Doll put him to bed. He remembers that he was frightened and wanted her to stay with him which she did until Uncle Bob came in to say goodnight. He heard his uncle whispering to his sister as he drifted off to sleep. He was woken by raised voices. It was his father and Uncle Bob and Aunt Doll arguing.

"You know why I can't take him."

"You could if you really wanted to. I suppose Eve isn't keen on starting married life with someone else's child."

"That's not fair, Bob."

"Nor is taking him away from all he's ever known. Especially now, for god's sake."

"I want him to be brought up by his family."

"What do you think that we've been doing all this time?"

"No, I mean my family."

"But he's hardly met them. We're his family too and we love him."

"Dorrie, it's like he's my own child."

"Sorry, but I've made up my mind."

"So, if you don't want to take him with you, what difference does it make if we take care of him instead? No fuss, no upheaval. He just stays here."

"He's my son."

"Not enough for you to want to look after him though." I want him to be a Daligan not a Hudson."

"What's wrong being a Hudson? Lou spent most of her married life thinking that changing her name hadn't really changed anything. Anyway, he's just a child, for god's sake."

17

"I just want him brought up by my family."

"Have you talked to him about it?

"No. Like you said, he's just a child."

"Dorrie, would you consider letting me adopt him?"

"No, I can't do that. That would mean giving him up."

"Instead of just not wanting him?"

"Enough. I don't want to talk about this anymore. I have to go back to my unit and it needs to be settled before I go."

"Why? You could just leave him with us until you have the chance to talk to Eve."

"I've enough on my plate with the army and arranging the wedding and I need this sorted out."

"You mean the wedding is already arranged?"

"Not the date but we're hoping for early in the new year."

"How could you? She's not even been buried yet."

"Look this is getting us nowhere. I've already talked to Ada and she'll take him."

"Ada and Bill?"

"Yes."

"How could you?"

"Well, I have and it's all arranged. Someone needs to take him to the Colleen Bawn on Sunday at 11. After that, you can come and collect him every Sunday and bring him here for a few hours. Ada has agreed to that."

"And that's it?

"Yes, I'm afraid it is. So will you tell Michael that I'll be round tomorrow morning before I leave?"

"You bastard. You selfish bastard."

"Mind your language, Bob."

"You'd make a saint swear. Now just leave. Please go. I don't want to ever see you again."

"I'm sorry that you feel that way. Doll, I'll see you tomorrow to make the final arrangements. Is that OK?"

"I suppose it'll have to be."

And with that, he walked out.
Then they heard a small child crying out.
    "It's OK, Michael, we're here."

"Doll, love, can you give me a few minutes. I'm not sure that I could hide my feelings in front of the boy".

"OK, Bob, Don't be long though. He'll be asking for you."

"Just two minutes?"

The next day, in full dress with Sam Browne belt, shoes and buttons polished, his father arrived at his mother in law's where Michael, Doll and Alice awaited him.
    "Michael, I'm sorry, my boy, I have to go back today but I will be back to see you soon."

"Can't I come with you, Daddy?"

"No, I'm sorry but the army needs me but I'll be back after Xmas when I'll have a surprise for you."

"What is it, Daddy?"

"Well, if I told you, it wouldn't be a surprise but I've left something in an envelope for your Xmas present. Auntie Doll can get you something. Doll?

"Of course. Do you need a cuppa before you go?"

"No, I need to get off and, perhaps it's best if I do."

"Michael, give your old dad a hug before I go."

Michael ran towards his father and wrapped his arms around the adult's legs before he was picked up and hugged.
"I don't want you to go. I want you to stay."

"Doll, please."

"Come on, Michael. Be a good boy. Remember, strong?"
He started to cry. "Why can't he stay? Why does he have to go?"

"Come on, little one. Let's go to the door and wave Daddy off. Then you and me can go to the park."

"But I don't want him to go."

"I know, my child. I know."
It took a while to stop him crying by which time his father was at the station waiting for the train. Life would be very different when they next met and that, too, would end in disappointment for him. As it always did where his father was concerned.
The following morning was the big adventure that his father had told him about. But why were Uncle Bob, Auntie Doll and his granny so sad? After breakfast (you need to eat it all up so that you won't be hungry) Uncle Bob took him out into the back garden to the swing he'd fixed to the cherry tree.

"Just a couple of swings, Michael, before you go."

"Why are you crying, Uncle Bob?"
"It's cold, Michael, and it's making my eyes water."

"Ready, Bob." It was Auntie Doll with a small suitcase in her hand. As he got off the swing, Uncle Bob hugged him and told him that he should be a good boy. Then he hugged him again; this time tighter than ever before. He was still crying.
"OK, Michael, off we go. It's only a short way."

"Where are we going, Auntie Doll?"

"We're off to see your Auntie Ada."
They took the same route that he and his father had until they got to Raymouth Road when they continued to Southwark Park Road until they got to the Colleen Bawn on the corner. And there was "Auntie Ada" waiting for them. Doll's face looked even more serious than it had before.
"Hello, Doll."

"Hello, Ada."

"Hello, Michael. Do you remember me? I'm your Auntie Ada."
He noticed that she was smiling and had kindly eyes.

"Look after him, Ada." It was Doll handing over the suitcase, "Here's all the stuff he needs."

"I will. Can Bob come round next Sunday at about 11 and back before it gets dark?"

"I'll tell him. See you then, Michael."
He could see that Aunt Doll was crying too and that just made it worse.
Ada reached out and took his hand from Auntie Doll then walked off with him past the Odeon Cinema. He tried to

pull away as he saw Auntie Doll walking off the way they'd just come but Ada held him fast.

"It's alright, Michael, you'll see her again next week." With that, Auntie Ada picked him up. He remembers that he was crying out for the familiarity that was walking away from him and then it's as if a set of shutters had come down. Yes, his Uncle Bob did come round on Sunday and took him home, except that it was his uncle's home and not his. That continued for a further three weeks until Bob stopped coming for him. "Too upsetting for the child" it would seem. The Hudsons and his mother were never mentioned again.

And, with that, his new life began, albeit without that which had been the centre of his universe. Living inside a shell in a world that was beyond a small child's ability to cope, somehow, he managed. It was to be almost a lifetime later that he understood just how abnormal was his normal.

From a close knit family living within a few streets of one another, his new family comprised his father's eldest sister and her husband, an elderly couple who were ill equipped to deal with a grieving child wrenched away from all he knew. Raking familiar streets was exchanged for a world circumscribed by a grey basement flat and dark, damp winter evenings. The sun had actually been extinguished. Yet he was a mere 15 minute walk away from all that he'd ever known. It might as well have been on the moon. The following summer, he and his cousins would be allowed to play in Southwark Park. He didn't realise it at the time but just five minutes beyond the gate, lived his mum's whole family. That particular journey was one that he wasn't to take again for another 45 years. By which time, of course, none of them were there anymore.

Not that he didn't have feelings, rather that he learned not to. So those shutters came into use whenever he needed them and he got on with his life. There is no memory of the grief he must have felt, of crying or unhappiness. Except something obviously did happen as he frequently wet the bed and soiled his pants. He can remember the ritual of the daily inspections, the razor strop being flexed and those shutters coming down, hard. Four more winters were to pass before that world changed. By which time, the child's psyche had formed based on an absence of nurturing, a certain resilience, an ability to survive and the theme of 'if only'. It was a template that was to determine his behavior for much of his adult life.

Inside the Shell

Arms reached out into empty space and came back empty. The child retreated into himself and got on with his life in his new home with the people that his father had left him with. What choice did he have? Those he needed weren't there to help so he didn't ask for any. There was no point. Instead, ignore the hole inside that she'd occupied and let the shell grow. Thicker, stronger, more protective. But not whole. Gaps in the plates. Gaps that people can see, if only they look. If they do look, though, they might feel the need to act and they're not really sure that they want to do that. So, hidden beneath that shell, the child waited. With little nurturing, empathy, that feeling for the plight of others, never developed. That which you don't experience, you don't learn. As he grew, however, manipulation, especially where women were concerned, did. This, and neediness, an unpleasant combination. No wonder later relationships never worked. Who wants a needy predator for a friend? Who wants to be what they can never be for someone when that person won't really let them in? So the child kept his head down and an adult quickly metamorphosed around him to deal with the situation. Little Michael and big Mike within the same body. That adult grew up caring for the child who lived quietly inside. Except that he didn't. The adult may have been on duty but the emotions were those of that five year old who never grew up. Always needy and aware of his 'aloneness', that which made him different to others. The naive question "But where's his mum?" with the emphasis on the third word, from a small child at a family party, something that reminded him, if ever he needed reminding. It wasn't a recipe for a healthy future.

Nobody's Child, later one of his favourite songs, he knew that he was different. Not friendless but knowing that, if you let people in, they hurt you, badly. What else had life taught him? So he became his own best friend and invented an invisible one as well. Adults don't care like you need them to. Another small person, someone he could talk to, could. Until, after a particularly realistic, bad dream, he left too. Let people in and they become friends. Then they leave. Does that include mum? Will she come back if I call for her? He soon found out that the answer was "No".

He's not sure how he survived but survive he did, albeit at some emotional cost. The most powerful of which was a belief that there had never actually been a mother. Literally. She had never existed. Defiance, resilience along with a certain stubbornness became second nature, along with a certainty that he was always to be right. Years later, someone told him that he must have had a shitty childhood. He received a sharp response. It wasn't for anyone else to judge, it was his life not theirs and, for him, it had been normal. It was to be almost a whole lifetime before he understood just how different it had been. By which time, he'd heard a song with the refrain which he related to completely:

"When I show you that I just don't care.
When I'm throwing punches in the air"

Four years after his mother died, he was rescued by another aunt and uncle but, despite their Herculean efforts, the die had been cast. Years later he realised just how much effort they'd put in to try to make things better. Unfortunately, it was too late, although the feelings that he has about them grow with the passing years. He knows what that feeling is but is unable to say the word. Fortunately, Gaynor, his wife tells him that they knew anyway and that makes him feel good.

Unfortunately, just as he was getting used to being part of a family, after his first ever letter, his father returned with his own new one in tow. What had been the child's dream became the young man's nightmare and, after six months of living with them, he was signed into the army at 15. There the shell just grew thicker still. A combination of the need to protect the child inside and the institutionalised bullying that prevailed made sure that he did. Yet, it just needed someone to respond for that young man to exhibit a caring side. Hence his early and ill considered first marriage, although that's another story.

Years later he undertook the long therapeutic journey which enabled him to put all those pieces of the jigsaw together; something that helped him to live his life with considerably less of that "if only" feeling. With that loosening of the carapace came the ability to let others in, even to form sustainable loving relationships. Crucially, it allowed a releasing of talents that he'd long dreamt of having. The child inside and the man outside have, almost, become one and the same person. And that feels good.

Over the years, the child grew into a man, albeit one with that small child's emotions locked inside the shell. The fact that his mother had never actually existed made any search for her unnecessary. Until mum's sister provided him with proof that she had been a real person. These took the form of a few photographs, the certificate his mother had been given when she registered his birth and a memorial card from the funeral. There were just three photographs, one of his mother as a young woman (the first one of her he'd ever seen), his parents' wedding photo and one of him in a pram with his mother and father in the back garden looking at the camera. Interestingly, the photo of the three of them together as a family had been torn in two and pasted back together. Such damage, probably after she received the letter, an expression of rage and despair.

Even with these, the illusion that his mother had never existed was one he never wavered from. A certainty he needed in order to keep the reality of her early death at bay.

Even the evidence itself was put away in a suitcase and forgotten; although ignored might be a better description. Until, many years later, a violent incident took place which, although he didn't realise it at the time, unlocked a door. In the meantime, 200 miles away from the scene of the incident, a cemetery that had been closed for many years, had reopened and two worlds were allowed to come together. The corporeal and the nether one. The former the one in which the man now lived and the latter, the afterlife, which his mother inhabited. It was to herald a meeting that both of them, in their own ways, had waited for longer than they could remember.

The Afterlife

For most, there is no after life. They just cease to exist and
gradually become indistinguishable from the background
that surrounds them. Eventually becoming part of it as their
bodies decay and merge with the soil from which new life
grows. They were either the lucky ones, who had died with
a modicum of peace (RIP), or those who may not have done
so but, gradually, gave up the struggle. These latter, by their
sheer weight of their languor, infecting those around them
so that the effort became beyond most of them. As for much
of humanity, life got in the way, except, in their case, it was
death that did that. Over a relatively short space of time
much of what they had been ceased to exist in any distin-
guishable form. They ceased to exist.

Then there were those in limbo, of which there were two
types. The 'Historic Ones' and the 'Unresolveds'. The former had been those who had, originally, been unresolved
but who, for whatever reason, had become trapped. Unable
to free themselves from their stasis, they wandered about
the immediate vicinity, scaring the natives and providing
a source of entertainment, opportunities for research and
a source of income for those still alive. Like some faulty
recording on repeat setting, they flickered into view for a

while only to shut down again until the next time the system demanded or allowed them to materialise. Some had been in this state for so long that they had little remembrance of who they had been or why they did what they did. They, in effect, became part of the fixtures and fittings; their existence helping to keep alive the belief in an afterlife that most of us will never know.

The 'Unresolveds', however, were those with a legacy of unfinished business. In combination with sufficient determination, stubbornness or anger to fight on, they did so, with one major proviso. They could only materialise, in bodily form, when called upon to do so by the object of their desire or when in the company of others of their kind. Such action being strengthened by that desire and the power of their will, alongside the unrequited needs of those left behind. Those who did this were few and far between. Confined by the location of their graves and, occasionally, by geography of their lives or deaths, they existed. They had awareness. Something that, obviously, died with the truly dead. In the cemeteries in which they were interred, they had knowledge of others in the locality, forming new relationships and, usually, becoming friends. Such friendships enabling them to become a small community of Unresolveds who could, literally, call on one another when needed. This, of course, included support to newcomers at a time when they most needed it. This ability also allowed them to materialise, in spirit only, when any of them just wanted to see what was happening in the outside world by watching visitors to the cemetery.

They existed alongside one another as best they could, through acquaintance, friendship, rivalry and all those things that had sustained them in life. The only difference was that they were now in limbo. Mostly they sustained themselves through a common purpose and their shared circumstances. And, it has to be said, a somewhat black humour; the 'humour of the veil'. They were also fairly blunt and would have little truck with 'asleep', 'passed away' or 'in the arms of'. They, after all, knew the reality. Not necessarily bleak but, certainly, in a state of a powerful unrequitedness and unmet desire.

Above all, they dreamt of reunion and whatever was the latest recipe for achieving that exalted status. For such it was. That thought of, once again, meeting whoever it was who was the source of so much yearning. There was no recognised procedure just a strength of feeling and the ability to sustain that over many years. Occasionally, word would come through, either as a direct call or extreme effort. Sometimes by an event of some significance. Usually they just waited. Their struggles unacknowledged until the call finally came. And, with it, a reunification and resolution of sorts. Not always, it has to be said, a happy one. Hence a begrudging acceptance of their lot. The joke among the more recent of them was that this wasn't 'Long Lost Families' but 'Long Dead Ones'. Left in limbo, they were the real ghosts. One such was his mother. One of a group of 'Unresolveds', the ghosts of popular fiction, there were just a few in Nunhead. Largely constrained within the cemetery walls, they formed a small community of those who waited.

This person, who her son had thought had given up had, he discovered, only done so physically and after a lifetime of ill health. The body no longer able to bear the years of sickness, pain and unhappiness. The spirit, however, was undiminished, nourished and sustained by the early removal from her only child. The upturned torch, so popular in the cemetery in which she was buried, the affirmation of a life ended before its time, was indeed apt. Above the graves, the flame may have been symbolically extinguished but below, for those ghosts, it, largely, remained undimmed. Something that could only be put out by resolution or acceptance. In the case of the latter, by a reunification with those they loved in life. Or the death of those loved ones.

So, having died of heart failure on 19 November 1947, Ada Louisa Daligan, nee Hudson, was interred on 25 November in grave number 42047. No tombstone was erected and the grave was grassed over some years later. Thanks to a kindly local authority officer, the grave was identified on 5 July 2012. As her son stood over the spot where she lay, he reflected that she was buried a mere six feet below; almost within touching distance. He remembers thinking that he hadn't been that close to her since the day she died 65 years previously. He later said that he'd never felt so at ease in his whole life. It felt like "home to me", the cue to another song; this one from his favourite, Randy Newman.

For her part, his mother had been there all that time. Patient in the surety that he would, one day, call out to her and that this action would be the first step towards their meeting. So few of them, the visit was sufficiently unusual that it was virtually the only topic of conversation for some days afterwards. It was to be another five years before he called her name and they met. In person, so to speak.

In the meantime, she waited in the knowledge that, if they didn't meet in what was left of her child's life, they would do so at the end of it. At which time, there would be a reunion and a resolution so that they could both rest in peace. So far she'd waited 70 years; a whole lifetime for most. So long that what were another few years in the great scheme of things? That thought, and the inevitability of their reunion, sustained her. That sense of history something that she'd passed on to her only child.

In Nunhead, where his mother lay and over 30 years since the last burial, there was what passed for excitement. One watching ghost had discovered that the cemetery was to be reopened. They would be joined by newcomers. How many would actually be in limbo and what news would they have? Obviously not many compared to the original 270,000 and mostly those were just dead. Among them, however, would be a few who were unresolved. New friends to be made and souls to be supported at this critical time for them. However, there was one noticeable difference from previous occupants; their diversity. A great change from before the cemetery was closed in 1969. So what, you might say, they're dead anyway. Well, some were just as likely to be prejudiced in limbo as they had been in life. Fortunately, sooner or later, they would see how utterly irrelevant that was in this new guise. After all, when you have, literally, nowhere else to go, it's likely that you will, eventually, make the best of it. And if you didn't? Well, it could get very lonely without the support of the few other ghosts that there were and life or, in this case, death, was bad enough without adding to it.

So, the Unresolveds of Nunhead would have to hone up on skills that they hadn't used for years hoping that, just maybe, some visitors or new occupants might have a link with any of them. In one case, it was to be, albeit for a short while. That young child was now a grown man with children of his own. After over 20 years of being separated from his mum's family, her sister, that Aunt Doll that he knew, had managed to contact him and they met. Following a divorce, she now ran a pub in Suffolk with her second husband, Bert. It was an amazing weekend after which he left with some mementoes of his mum and details of where she was buried. Which is why, when the cemetery was reopened, he could be found, map in hand, looking for her grave.

It was also when one of the other ghosts, on watch, saw him near to where his mum was buried. The fact that someone was looking near where one of their own lay was of obvious import. Beneath his feet, sensing his presence, his mother materialised, albeit in spirit form only. Unaware of her presence and to her utter frustration, in the deep undergrowth and with no headstone to guide him, he left without achieving his objective. She was inconsolable for days. So much so that she determined that she had to do something even if, as she'd been warned, it wouldn't work. What she hadn't allowed for was her anger.

He'd recently moved to London and, with his most recent relationship over, was living on his own. In these circumstances, a late night drink or two always helped him to sleep so he adjourned to the local. A couple of pints later and he was back home, still unable to sleep. At which point, he tried watching some late night TV before turning in. The dream, when it materialised, was so vivid as to be more than just a nightmare. So much so that he awoke to with a start to see a female figure just by the doorway to the kitchen. Slim and dark haired, she was wearing what appeared to be a white wedding dress. As he watched, this became a shroud and the flesh on her face was replaced by maggots crawling through her eye sockets. He sat up in bed, very frightened, before getting up to turn the light on. The light stayed on and he remained awake for much of the rest of the night. His mother, in the meantime, was back in her grave unaware of the fright that she'd given her son but conscious of the fact that she hadn't achieved her goal. That would remain some years into the future.

The new millennium found him married again and with a new daughter, although still with that feeling that the life he wanted wasn't for the likes of him. Maybe it was the sense of a new life in front of him that provided the impetus or, maybe, it was just age, but he decided that he really did need to find the grave. Restoration work, including removal of all the knotweed, was nearly complete and now seemed as good a time as any.

By this time the cemetery had become a place of some renown and one that he and his wife visited occasionally. So, in July 2012, they took the journey across London to identify the plot. Unfortunately, that area had still not been properly cleared but, thanks to the good offices of a local authority officer on duty, coincidentally also Michael, they were successful. He can still remember the feeling of ease and peace that he felt when he stood over where she was buried. Unfortunately, his mother, only six feet away could only assume spirit form and watch, helpless and frustrated. Still, at least she now knew how the child looked and that he seemed settled. It was to be another few years before he finally made the call. She had waited long enough already, so what was a little longer. He'd finally taken that first step so the next one, the one that would unite them, would surely follow.

The Arrival

His first thoughts were that he was still dreaming. Yet, even with his eyes open, he could hear a voice in his head. And it was insistent.

Michael, you need to ask me to come in. Just call my name.
The words then grew stronger.

Michael, please, you need to call me.
Somehow he knew who it was.

Why did you go? Why did you give up when I needed you?

Please, Michael, just call my name.

No! You left, not me. You need to come to me. Is that too much to ask?

Again, more insistently. *Please, that's all you have to do.*

No!

Michael, please. You only have to say my name.

Then, suddenly, it burst out.

"Mum, why couldn't you stay, wasn't I enough for you? Where are you?"

There he'd said it!

The room grew warmer, more comfortable and he was no longer alone. Someone was with him. Strong but hurt with an overwhelming feeling of love, of the need to care.

"Mum?"

"Michael."

And there she was after all those years. Just like her 1940's photo. How could this be when she was dead? Dark hair, dark eyes and full lips. The latter like the granddaughter born nearly 50 years after she'd died. Smaller than he'd imagined and very slim but without the hat that she was wearing in the photo that he has. She was smiling at him.

"Mum, is it really you? How can that be?"

"Of course it is, my child. Who did you think it was?"

"But you're dead."

"Ten out of ten for the young man at the front of the class."

He shook his head and smiled. In his wildest imaginings, he long dreamt about this without thinking that the encounter would be a humorous one.

He sat up in bed to move towards her before realising that he needed his dressing gown. He pointed towards where it was hanging on the back of the door.

"I'm sorry but could you pass that to me?"

It was then that she burst into laughter.

"Michael, I bathed you for the first five years of your life. There's nothing that I haven't already seen."

He smiled back at the thought that, at least, this daughter of the Hudson family seemed to have as earthy a sense of humour as his father's sisters.

"Maybe not but I'd feel happier with something on."

As he put it on, their hands touched. The touch quickly became a clasp; the physical touch something that he could never have imagined. Then a pulling together and an embrace that was warm and human in its envelopment but also deeply needy. He'd always watched *Long Lost Families* but that was for the living. This person had been dead for 70 years!

Eventually they both let go and stepped back from one another. Laughter and tears combining while they feasted their eyes with what was in front of them. Then they hugged again. It was as if the rest of the world no longer existed, that feeling of being with someone who had a relationship with you that no one else could ever have; that of mother and child.

In this case with the unique twist that this time it was an old man and his, now, much younger mother. It really was J M Barrie's Mary Rose made real. This, occasionally, abrasive person suddenly felt very shy. What to say after all these years? Other than "Hello, Mum", so softly as to be almost inaudible.

She smiled, "Hello, Michael."

He could no longer hold back the tears and neither could she. Another embrace with each of them drawing strength from the other's emotions, from their enclosure of one another. Did it get any better than this? Without thinking that he was talking to someone who wasn't alive, he said,

"Do you mind if I get dressed and you wait in the living room, it's more comfortable."

"Of course not. Lead on, my child."

Please sit down" he said, indicating the sofa before having a quick wash and putting on some clothes.

As quickly as he could he followed her.

"I can't believe this is happening. It's something that I've dreamt about all my life."

"I've dreamt of it for all of my death". This in the south London twang he'd long since dropped.

As they broke into laughter, he thought "Well, at least we share the same sense of humour".

But not the same accent.

"What took you so long?"

"It's a long story, Mum, and one we can talk about for however long we've got."

How do you heal a lifetime of yearning? You can't, although you can live in the present. Do the dead have a future as well as a past?

As if to read his thoughts, she said, "I'm here now, Michael".

"Yes, but for how long?" Always his refrain in any relationship.

"I'm not really sure".

"You mean that you might leave again?"

"Eventually, yes but not straight away and, certainly, not until we've had the chance to make up for what we've missed out on for all those years."

"So, you're a ghost? I don't believe in ghosts."

"Well," she laughed again, "this must be quite a shock for you then."

As he heard her laugh, he was instantly transported, back to a time before she'd become really ill and they were a small child and his mother together in Edale Road. Little did he then know what lay ahead. Shaking his head, he smiled back. "Mum, how is this possible and after so long?"

"It's simple really. I'm one of the unresolved, a ghost. And I will be until you and me have had the chance to get to know one another and can part with some sort of ease. I'm then resolved and no longer have to exist in limbo. "

"And then?"

"It seems that I die just like I would have done in normal circumstances."

"But why now?

"Michael, I've tried for years but you were so damaged by what had happened that there was no chance. Now, there is. You getting older, me realising that I have less time to try and, of course the anniversary."

"The anniversary and the fact that the council have finally cleared the area so that I can reach your grave, friends of mine dying, I should have thought…."

"Well we're together now, my child, so let's make the most of it."

"Amen to that, Mum. But what happens then?"

"As far as I know, that's it. No unresolved has ever come back to let us know."

"One last thing. Any idea how long we've got?"

"Michael, I've only just got here.
Not long. Usually until the anniversary of the burial. I think. I can only go on the experience of what I've heard from the others and that's not much."

"Can we prevent it happening?"

"It seems not. Anyway, why are we talking about this when I've only just got here?"

"Sorry, Mum, but my childhood has left me with a need to know but you're right. Let's make the most of it."
At this point, the traditional family offering, to welcome visitors, would have been a cup of tea and a slice of cake. Do ghosts eat?
She, of course, knew the ritual. After all, where had he learned it from?
"You have a cuppa if you want, I don't eat or drink, much as I would love to right now. The need for some rituals can carry on even when you're no longer alive."
She smiled at a remembrance of what had been. As she did

he walked into the kitchen, looking back as he did so. Just in case.

"It's OK I'm not going anywhere."

You bloody did last time.

A thought that the adult blocked before the words formed. Quite an achievement that.

As he made the tea, the questions came thick and fast in his head. He, very obviously wasn't dreaming so, how had she got here? What if they didn't like one another? Would she understand that he'd grown up during the past 70 years. He may be her son but he was no longer her baby. Do ghosts feel the passing of time and how could she be warm?

As if to read his mind, she said, "We have so much to talk about, Michael." Nobody but her had ever called him that. She looked around. "So this is where you live. You have done well for yourself, haven't you, my boy?"

"We like it."

"The three of you?"

"How did you know that?"

"I managed to get a fleeting visit soon after your new daughter was born. Ellie, isn't it? The feelings were so strong that it just happened although I didn't have the strength or the concentration to stay."

"So that was you? Gaynor, my wife, told me that she'd felt something brush past her as she was bathing Ellie. She said that whatever it was felt very caring and protective."

A big smile crossed her face. "Yes that was me. I thought she'd noticed. It was lovely to see my new granddaughter, even if it was for such a very short time. It was awful being dragged back but some of the others had had similar experiences and they helped enormously. "

"That was nearly 25 years ago."

"Doesn't time fly when you're enjoying yourself."

"Yes, doesn't it." As they both burst out laughing. He was already getting to like this person.

"I take it they're both at work right now?"

"No, they've gone to see Nancy, Gaynor's mum, in Derbyshire. They'll be away a few more days."

"Will I get the chance to meet them then?"

"As long as I can call you back, you will."

"So that should work out OK then." She didn't want to say anymore about duration at the moment so covered it up by asking what they did.

"Well, Gaynor is a teacher, although now part time, and Ellie works as an Office Manager for a bookseller but I guess that they'd like to tell you about themselves when you meet. Is that OK?"
She looked around her. "Of course. Anyway aren't you going to show your old mother around?"

"I'd love to, although it shouldn't take very long and watch out for Midnight, the cat."

"Why? Doesn't she like strangers?"

"Well, she's a little wary and she is getting on a bit. It's just that I thought that, cats and ghosts, you know?"

"I understand that they might have a sixth sense but I think that's about all."

"Oh, OK."
So, like any other son, he showed his mother around where he lived with a mixture of pride and awkwardness. The garden, especially, was a particular delight. Fortunately, he'd done the weekly clean yesterday so, at least, it was tidy. True to form, the cat was asleep in his daughter's room and, also

true to form, hardly stirred. His mother, in her turn, experienced similar feelings to her son, as well as a curiosity at the level of household technology. The majority of which hadn't even been thought of when she was alive. As the questions tumbled out and the explanations provided, the curiosity was replaced with awe and disbelief. Something that even practical demonstrations did little to allay. In the end, they both had to settle for the reality, although he noticed that she still bore a look of bemusement some while later.

By this time, his tea was cold and a fresh cup had to be made. At this she smiled as she thought about the number of times her own tea must have got cold while she catered for his needs as a small child. Some things never change although the roles may be reversed. He put his fresh cup down and sat on the sofa next to her. How many times had he dreamt of this happening, but where to start? Well, the obvious, and one he'd long ago pushed to the back of his mind, might be a good place.

"I've missed you."

"I've missed you too. Look at you now. Are you happy?"

"I am now although it's taken much of my life to get there. Haven't you been able to see it all from wherever you are? Or should that be were?"

"No, those of us who "live in limbo" just exist. We don't see everything other than in the immediate vicinity."

"How does it feel?"

"You get used to it and it's not that bad. The real difference is that life had a purpose. As a ghost, my purpose is to get to the situation where I'm OK about letting go. And, at last, I've got the chance to do just that. Whether it will be easy to actually let go, I'm not so sure."

"But what do you do? Does anything happen?"

"Not a great deal, although once we've learnt the ropes,

we can materialise in spirit and listen in to those who visit the cemetery. Especially during funerals and other events."

"Are there many like you?"

"I only know the ones in Nunhead and, no, there aren't too many of us. Perhaps twenty or so. Along with the odd new one."

"Can those alive see you?"

"No, that's why I said "in spirit". It takes this, you calling, for me to materialise to those still alive."

"But why now?"

"Michael, are you so unaware of what day it is?"

"No, of course not."

"Well anniversaries like that act as a reminder and make the pull stronger. While anniversaries of funerals can pull harder in the other direction. And, as you who're still alive get older, well, you know."

"But how are you warm?"
Michael, do you always have to ask awkward questions and at the bloody wrong time?
She, however, had no intentions of letting anything spoil the occasion. "It seems that I'm driven by emotion both to get me here in the first place then to keep me here. The intensity of that makes me warm and keeps me that way. Until, it all seems to run down towards the very end when it's difficult to sustain and as it dies off, my visit will come to an end. Until, of course, when you call me again. Like tomorrow and the day after. Although you have to give both of us the time to recover so, perhaps, not too often each day."

"This isn't just a one off then?"

"No, we continue until I'm resolved."

"Who decides when that is?"

"Unfortunately neither of us. Just like getting older, it happens and then you die."

"But you've already done that once."

"Yes, I have but not properly. This time I think I will." He could see it was something that she needed to face up to, so saying it was her way of doing that. He could also see that she'd wished that she hadn't been quite so blunt. Another trait that he'd inherited. He looked into her eyes and took her hands in his.

"We'll think about that nearer the time, shall we?"

"Yes, my son, let's do that." She smiled.

"You do know that I've been to the cemetery to look for the grave, don't you?"

"Of course. It was very frustrating that you didn't call me but I felt you there and watched you. The first time many years ago when were with a young woman looking for where I'm buried, then other times when you just visited. And, finally, that time with Gaynor when you actually stood over where I am."

"Yes, we do visit. Nunhead is a bit of a wonderland for me. It's as if nature has taken over. I love that. Actually identifying where you were and just standing over you was one of the most amazing feelings I've ever had. Like nothing I'd ever experienced before. You were only six feet away and I was utterly at peace."
She smiled, "What took you so long?"

"I ask myself that question, although it seemed natural at the time not to try. You'd died and you were never

43

mentioned again so I learnt to get on with life. In that process, you got forgotten. I'm sorry."

She looked at him with a very sad expression on her face. It was as if she was in great pain and he couldn't help but reach out to her.

"It wasn't your fault, my child and, OK, it was a long time coming but we have now and how many people get to experience this." That smile again. "What I don't understand, though, is how you found me in the first place."

"That goes back a long way to when Aunt Doll got in touch when I was in my early 20's and we met. She and Bert had a pub in Debenham in Suffolk."

"Bert, what happened to Freddie?"

"He and Doll got divorced and she moved in with Bert. Anyway, when we met, she gave me a photo of you, the first one I'd ever seen. She also gave me a memorial card and some information on where you were buried in Nunhead. After many years, I got in touch with the council and they provided all the details. I went to see Doll again after her and Bert moved to another pub, near Brighton, to be near David and his family. His wife, Margaret, was a medium and Doll wanted to get in touch with you. She said you'd be waiting. Unfortunately, we all had a bit too much to drink and it never happened."

"Doll and David, you and me. That would have been something."

"Yes, it would. Mind you I didn't keep in touch, as usual. Doing that never seemed important. Until now."

When he looked up, his mother looked wistful. He reached out and held her hands again.

"Sorry, Mum. There were so many things I should have done but opening old wounds always hurt so I kept them covered."

"How bad was it?"

"I'm not really sure. I got by. It's just that, as I get older, I realise what I've missed."

"Well, you're here now, so let's just enjoy it for what it is."

"I'll second that. Now, tell me about you. What do you actually do?"

"Well, there's not much to tell. Most of the time we're like cats. We just sleep, if that's the right word. We talk to those who're like us in the cemetery. Not the dead because they're dead. Just those in limbo. Or just close our eyes and drift into nowhere. It's pleasant enough. At least we don't have to worry about practicalities, like money. That was something that made me sick with worry, especially towards the end. Once your father had his divorce, we would have had hardly any money coming in and I wouldn't have been able to pay the rent. My mum wasn't well and was overcrowded anyway, so I was worried that we'd be on the streets."

"I know, I have vague memories of you crying about that and that fear of losing my home has been with me for most of my life. Thanks, Dad."

"Are you angry about him?"

"I never used to think that I was. He never figured in my life so he wasn't important. Even when he did turn up, he always made things worse, every time, without fail. So, why should I be angry? What I am angry about is what might have been. Still, I know what I have done and that sustains me. With a vengeance I might add."
She lowered her gaze, "Maybe if I'd behaved differently…"

"Mum, you had no hand in making him the person that he was."

"Yes, but…"

"No, Mum, you tried." And, for the first time in his life, there came the realisation of her feelings for that small child. He dropped back onto the sofa exhaling as he did so.

"Michael, what's wrong? Are you alright?"
He looked at her and smiled, "Never better." The grin grew wider.

"What happened?"

"Mum, I often have, what I call, my 'penny dropping moments'. When, almost in a flash, something that should have been blindingly obvious, suddenly occurs to me. And that was one of them."

"Are you going to tell me what or do I have to guess?" This in a, half jokingly, strict voice.

"I just had a half memory of how good it felt when you were happy."
She blushed. "You made me so, my child."

"Sorry, Mum, I hadn't realised. I'm so sorry" His voice dropped away as he looked down.

"Michael, we're together now and that's the important thing."
Again that smile only this time a little weary.

"It's funny how I kept that anger at bay for so long, mainly by erasing my father from my life. Even now, the thought of any physical contact with him makes me feel uncomfortable."

"Although I loved your father very much, I think that it does with me now. Still, as they say, 'water under the bridge.'"

"I'm just sorry that so much of your life, and mine as a child, was affected by illness. Was it always the same?"

"Well, I'd never been that well ever since the rheumatic fever as a child. And I smoked. We all did in those days but it didn't help. And being pregnant made me weary. It wasn't planned but, once it happened, the family rallied round to make up for Dorrie's absence. And, as Doll said, "At least you're having your husband's child." There would be a few who would have some explaining to do when the war ended. She smiled at the memory. "Anyway, your arrival became the centre of attention in the family for a while; despite their reservations. I was taken into St Olave's early just as a precaution. You have to remember that, in those days, child-birth wasn't easy and, after a long labour, you came into the world on the Monday afternoon. I was kept in for a while but, eventually, they let me come home and I stayed at my mum's until I got my strength back."

"So, were you OK then?"

"Well, like any mother, having a baby wasn't easy but the family mucked in and we got by. I took you round to meet your father's family. Just in time really as Ada, your father's mother, died later that year. Somehow Dorrie managed to get compassionate leave for the funeral. I could tell then that the war had changed him as it did for all of us. Anyway, he went back and that was an awful time. I managed but the bombing continued, although not as bad as before, and the war showed no sign of ending. Looking back, it's all a bit of a blur. The bombs, limited rations, queues, no husband, you to care for and no end in sight. It all got to me. Then, finally, your father's letter. Doll was right, I gave up and I'm sorry, my child. You deserved better."
He shook his head at her, "You did your best, Mum, and look at me now. That wouldn't have happened without you."
She smiled back, "It would help if I could believe that, Michael."

"The proof, as they say, of the pudding is in the eating and my family and friends think that the 'afters', the rest of my life, have been quite good."

"The doctors tried to help but, at the end, I did go down-hill fast. Finally, I was too ill to care. I'm sorry but, I was just too weak to carry on. Then I had some sort of kidney infection and my arms and legs swelled up."

"Your death certificate was signed by Dr Richardson and he put congestive cardiac failure, mitral stenosis and nephritis as the causes. I checked and the stenosis can be caused by rheumatic fever and nephritis was that kidney infection."

"Yes me and my sister Alice, Lally, both had rheumatic fever as children. It gave us heart problems and she died when she was 33. My mum looked after her kids. I lasted a year more. Doctor Richardson was our local doctor and he always was very thorough."

"That's the word a doctor friend of mine said when he read the certificate. What I can't begin to imagine though, Mum, is what it must have been like but, maybe it's best if we don't go there."

"Amen to that, my child."
The adult agreed with that although the child inside was less forgiving.
Wasn't I good enough? Ask her that.
I can't, it would be unkind. Anyway she tried hard.
She left me when I needed her.
She couldn't help it and, anyway, I was there for you.
But she wasn't.
It wasn't her fault.
Well, it wasn't mine, was it?
No, but I thought that we'd sorted this out.
You might have done but you're not me.
No, but I am what you become.
Will I grow up too?
You have done except you just haven't realised it yet.
I don't want to grow up. I just want to be happy. Not to be scared.
You don't have to worry, she's here for both of us. Now, please be quiet.

48

Spoilsport!

At which point, he decided that, before this ended, he would abrogate himself from this particular responsibility. After all, a lifetime of caring for someone is a long time in anyone's book especially when the person you're caring for doesn't really exist. Anyway he was enjoying his time with this ghost and didn't want another unresolved personality spoiling it. Even if it was his own.

"Are you alright, Michael?"

"Yes, Mum, just things I have to keep reminding myself."

"Anything I should know?"

"No, it's fine. Life is good for me. I have most of the things that I want and I still have things I want to do. This, us meeting, really is the icing on the cake. Who could have imagined that something like this would ever happen?"

"Well, I have the upper hand on that one as I knew that it could, I just wasn't sure that it would. It's a dream come true and one that enables me to put a few ghosts to rest." This with big grins. First hers then his. His with a shake of the head at her wicked sense of humour.

"Have you been blaming yourself all this time?"

"Probably. When I saw you that last time, my heart broke. I couldn't stay and your father seemed more interested in his new woman."

"Mum, it's OK. I'm not saying that there weren't some bad times. There were lots of them and sometimes they were very bad. But I survived them all and I've ended up in a good place. Fortunately my family, especially my kids, have sustained me. Anchored me, if you like. The first two at an age when they weren't really old enough to do so. But, now is good. So, please, no regrets. Anyway, I don't want it to spoil our time now. We've both waited long enough as it is."

It was then that the simple act of drinking tea in her

company reminded him, if he ever needed it, of a closeness that had been absent for most of his life and what he really had missed.

"Mum, there's so much I want to ask but first of all, some things I don't understand."

"I can imagine that there might be. So what are they?"

"Well, for a start, what happens when you die?"
She laughed. "You never stopped asking questions when you were small so I should have expected this. Do you have anything particular in mind?"

"I'm sorry, Mum, but I've never been in this position before. Not of talking to a ghost, you understand, but just talking to you, my mother. I've never been that good at making conversation without there being something to discuss. Even, sometimes, with people that I love. It's something that I've had to learn and there's a lot I want to know so the questions might not all come out in the way that I want them to."
She smiled. "Yes I know. We have to get to know one another after an absence of, how long?"

"70 years. Also, I was a small child then and you were an adult. Now I'm older than you!"

"You're still my child, Michael, and that will never change."

"No, I know that and it's a very special feeling, But it is one that I might have to get to understand. That of growing up with your parents, with all their faults, instead of idealising them."

"Have you idealised me, then?"

"I don't know although I do understand that I never knew what you were like or what it was like to have a mum and dad bring you up. If it never did before, it hit me when I met Graham, my Aunt Eileen's son, a few years back. He told me that he could remember being at a party at Aunt Ada's when

he asked his mum, "But where's his mum." The fact that
he couldn't understand why I didn't have a mum brought it
home to me over 60 years later."

"I'm sorry, my son, that I couldn't be there for you."

"Don't be silly, mum, it wasn't your fault. Even as a small
child, I realised that you were very ill.
In fact that was the background noise to my childhood. I've
read up on it since and found out that, in those days dropsy
wasn't treatable. So let's make the best of something that
doesn't happen to many people in this world. I might even
write a book about it one day!"
They both laughed.

"OK, my child, ask away."

"Well, what was it like when you died?"

"From what I remember, very strange. I'd expected what
I'd been brought up to believe. Heaven, St Peter, angels
and the pearly gates. Somewhere where I wouldn't be sick
anymore and everything would be lovely. I also knew what
the alternative was but felt that I hadn't done anything bad
enough to warrant that."
His younger self would have made some sharp comment but,
fortunately, he'd left that person behind some time ago and,
anyway, this was his mother.

"And?"

"Then Doll and Ann laid me out and that wasn't nice at
all. They were more embarrassed than I would have been if
I'd not been dead."
He tried not to smile at the thought.
"Mum, you won't know but a good few years ago I
decided that it was time that I tried to trace my family so I
wrote a letter to the South London Press. One of the people
who got in touch was a cousin, Jean."

"Jack's daughter. Well I never did."

"Yes. She said that she'd been in the house when you died and remembers that happening. It horrified her."

"Like I said, it wasn't very nice but it was a very long time ago. Then I was put in the coffin and laid out in the front room."
She hesitated and it was as if a chill had descended on the two of them.
"Then it was as if I was still there. Watching, drifting in and out of things. I saw you all in the front room looking at me. It broke my heart especially when they brought you in to say goodbye."
The chill became a fear as it brought back that 'whales teeth' memory. It took all his effort not to cry.
"Mum, do you mind if we skip that bit?"

"OK, my child but do you really not remember me at all?"

"Mum, I'm really sorry but no."

"Oh." She looked very sad as she shook her head and he waited for her to continue.
"Then I was at the cemetery looking down on you and that was even worse."

"Than being in a coffin?" said the person he had been.

"Michael!"

"Sorry, mum. My response has always been to make light of things. It makes it easier to cope. Please go on."

"Then you all left and it went dark again. More than just dark, it was as if I was semi conscious. No feelings and drifting. Something I've learned to get used to over the years. Needless to say, it was very frightening. Fear of the unknown seems to be deep rooted."

"Even when you're dead and actually in the unknown?"

"It's just a matter of degree, Michael."
How many times had he heard himself say that over the years?

"You see, I knew that I was dead and that was bad enough but where was I? Why weren't there angels to meet me and make sure that I was alright? It was just very frightening and not what I'd been led to believe."
He nodded and thought that, perhaps, now wouldn't be a good idea to bring his own views on religion."
She noticed his hesitation, "Michael, don't you go to church?"

"No." Was the best he could offer at this time before adding, quickly, "So where were you?"

"I didn't know which made it worse. I later discovered that, in fact, I was in limbo. Then I heard voices. People whispering. That was even more scary until I made out what they were saying.

"It's OK, love. Don't worry, we're here. You'll be OK. Just relax."

"I managed to open my eyes and tell them that my name was Lou. Lou Daligan. It was then that I realised that I wasn't in the coffin anymore but in the company of others. About half a dozen of them, some more solid than the rest. They looked like what I'd imagined that ghosts might look like, only more alive. All of them older than I was, probably around fifty or sixty years old. All women. They introduced themselves as Ada, Margie, Thora, Gladys, Ellen and Sylvie. Their names very reminiscent and something that put me at ease or, at least, more at ease than I'd been. Not that that would have been difficult. The introductions over, they sat down next to me and set about explaining to me the world that I now inhabited. First by answering my questions and then by showing me around. Not that we could go very far and certainly not beyond the cemetery gates. It was then that I found out that I was a ghost, one of the unresolved, and what that meant. I learnt that my more solid form, at least compared to theirs, was created by my afterlife newness but, largely, by my emotional strength. My rage at being torn away from you so early in life. They, by contrast, were slightly faded although, as they adjusted to the situation, they became more solid.

They were clothed as they had been in life and spoke as they would normally have done. Despite the wierdness of the situation. These things were a real comfort to me and helped me to feel more at ease. The fact that they were all women, older than I was (if that's the right way to describe the situation) made me feel as if it was my mum and her sisters that I was talking to. It helped enormously. It took a while but, gradually, I became less frightened. Indeed, it didn't take too long before I got to know them well and became one of them. It's funny really how you can get used to something that is beyond your comprehension even for those of us who believe. It's as if my mind somehow managed to become bigger and think in other ways."

"It's what my generation would call a change in your mindset, how you see things. Mind you, learning how to be dead would be a pretty amazing one."

"Looking back, I can see that it was but, now it's as if I've always felt this way."

"I know what you mean. After many years of therapy to get myself sorted out, I look back on the life that I used to have as one that someone else lived. Yet I know that that person was still me."

"Therapy? You mean Freud?"

"Yes, Mum, it's a long story but, basically, I talked to someone who helped me to get to the root of my problems and sort them out."

"Did it work?"

"You bet it did and, when we have more time, I'll tell you about it. Anyway, back to you. It's been 70 years since you died. Have you been aware all that time?"

"I'm not sure how to explain this but it's not like being alive."

"I'd rather gathered that."

"No, what I mean is that when I lived, there were always things to do. You got up in the morning and did things until it was time to go to bed. We had little money and life was a struggle, for everyone. As kids we often went to bed hungry. So the lives we led were determined by those circumstances. It's the way that it was and has always been for people like us. We knew that and just got on with it. My dad worked in butchering, your Uncle Bob worked in the Docks on the floating timber, your grandfather and his father were coopers. So was your dad until be joined the army. We didn't expect anything else. Mind you, your Uncle Lal knew that life could be different. He was very angry about it but knew that things wouldn't change much in his lifetime."

"It's funny, Mum, but they actually did. He saw those changes for his children. They went to grammar school and had greater expectations. The generation that fought in the War was determined that life would be different afterwards and, at least for a long while, it was."

"You sound as though you have the same anger as Lal?"

"Well it had to pass onto someone. Perhaps losing you and seeing other children with their mums and dads made me see that things were different for me. It's always driven me, that dream of a better world; one that could be. So I created my own little world; one that I could live in irrespective of what happened outside. It was like a bubble that I took with me wherever I went and, later, one that I created

55

in my work. However, much as I'd like to talk about my life, right now, I want to know about you."

"What, apart from the fact that I've spent the past 70 years waiting?"

"Yes, I know, I could have called earlier but you were dead and I never thought that this was possible. Much as I dreamt about it often. If only I'd known......"He laughed.
"My whole life has been "if only! So, what do you actually do?"

"You do, as you describe it, while you're alive. Those who are dead no longer exist and us 'Unresolveds', well we exist and we wait."

"Isn't that boring?"

"As I said, cats sleep for most of their lives and are they bored?"

"No, but they don't do anything much either."

"Neither do we. You see, time no longer passes for us as it does for you. Except when we're in our bodies. And that only happens in situations like this. Barring the occasional accident, of course." She smiled.

"Accident?"

"Well, they do happen. Either we materialise in the wrong place or one of us is in a mischievous mood with those who try to get through to us."

"You mean at seances?"

"Not always"

"Have you ever scared any of the natives?"

"No, Michael, I was brought up to behave properly."
At which, she smiled.

"Mind you, there were times when I thought about putting the fear of God into your father. Not that he'd called me properly just when he'd had a bit to drink and felt sorry for himself, he'd talk to me in his imagination."

"What did you say?"

"Nothing. He hadn't called me."

"Weren't you tempted?"

"Yes I was but there wasn't enough to get through and it would have been wrong. Mind you, it was good to hear the word "sorry" even if he was drunk."

"So you can get through without a direct call, say, from someone like me? Someone close."

"Yes, like at the funeral when there was overwhelming emotion. I can't be involved but I can watch."

"But not in your body?"

"No, not in my body. Also, it seems, for me, the call has come from you. I suspect that that's because I feel unresolved because of having to leave you as a child. Certainly, once I'm with you, the strength of feeling from others helps me to stay."

"Anyway, I wouldn't have appeared in that way even if I could as it wouldn't have been right to add to the grief with the shock of actually seeing a ghost."

"But you ghosts can talk to one another?"

"Yes, but only those nearby. We seem to feed off one another to do that."

"And you can watch the outside world?"

"Yes, we can but only those within the cemetery and normally only in spirit. There seem to be limits of our range and abilities. It can also be sad as it is a reminder of what they were. Without, of course, most of the physical things that afflict those who are alive. Hunger, pain, illness and the rest."

"But still with the emotions?"

"Well, you learn to live with them but, yes, we still have emotions. Ghosts are sustained by emotion. And we learn to develop what you called a different mindset. One with no responsibilities and no expectations. Although we do have hope."

"It's funny, I've travelled in the other direction. In the life I used to lead I didn't have expectations or hope. As I started to get myself sorted out, the expectations came along. So much so that I want to leave some small mark. That's one of the reasons I write."

"You write books?" She looked shocked.

"Yep. Four so far."

"Who'd have thought that my child would write books."

"Your child certainly didn't for more years than he can remember. Now he knows he can and that he's good at it. Like I said, I might even write a book about you and me." She smiled at the thought. Their time together in a book. Now that thought would be something to take back to the others.
It was then that he noticed that, in his usual way, he hadn't realised that this might be making his mum feel uncomfortable.
"You OK, Mum?"

"I am but I'm reminded of how scary those first hours were. You see then I was only recently deceased and was alone. It would have been easier if I'd just been dead. Then I'd just have ceased to exist. But, no, my separation from you prevented that. I was very frightened. Until I heard those voices and saw people talking to me. That was also very frightening as I had no idea of where I was or who they were. They comforted me and explained what was happening and why. The fear and anger died down and I, too, accepted the fact that I was a ghost. After a while, some of them went back to their dead time while others stayed to help me through those first days until I was ready to join them. They all knew how frightening that would be so they helped me to get used to it."

"Did that take long?"

"It didn't seem like it although I'm not sure. Although we are aware that time passes, we don't have quite the same, detailed, sense of that that you do. Just like you when you're asleep, you have no sense of time, so we don't when we're "at rest". Obviously, when we materialise, we do but that's usually for short interludes."

"How did you learn to do that?"

"Again, just like when you were a child, you learnt things from me. Well, I also learned from the others. It's actually quite easy although sustaining it can be very tiring."

"Is this?"

"I suspect that it will be and we'll both know when that is."

"You mean now or in the longer term?"

"Both, I think."

"I'm not sure that I like the sound of that"

"I don't like the thought of it but we need to make the best of what we have, so……."

"You're right, mum. I don't want to think about it so let's not." He knew that this was wishful thinking but it was his only defence and not a very successful one at that.

"Do you mind if I ask you something now, my child?"

"Sorry, Mum, I should have thought."

"Well, how were you?"

"To be honest, I think I've shut it out completely as I have no memory whatsoever although I do have feelings about being on my own. It's something that's stood me in good stead over the years, though. At least I think it has."

"What do you mean?"

"Well, I've always been happy in my own company and I do like to do things for myself, in my own way."

"Yes, I remember. You were always a child who did things your own way. I suspect that, because I was so ill, you had no choice. I used to think "That's my boy" while feeling sad that I wouldn't be around to watch you grow up."

"I can't imagine how that must have felt but I think I felt that too."

"What do you mean? You knew that I was dying?"

"No, because I'm not sure that a child can have that sort of awareness. But it was a central issue in my childhood and all your family knew about it. I'm sure I picked up on that. I also remember you used to sing, "You are my sunshine.""

"Yes, when your father wrote to say he wanted a divorce. I'd waited long enough to get him and now he wanted to marry that other woman. I'm sorry that all this happened,

Michael. I never wanted any of it."

"Mum, none of it was your fault and, yes, not having a mother (and a father) around has affected my whole life but, as the saying goes, 'Look at me now!' So let's make the best of what we have. OK?"
The sadness was still there even as she nodded and reached out to hold his hand.

"So, being a ghost?"

"It's difficult because like you, my other life seems like that of a different person. I was, after all, alive and was a wife (at least for a while), a daughter, a sister, an aunt, a cousin, a friend and, most of all, I was a mother. Do you know what it feels like to give birth, Michael? And do you know what it feels like to die and leave your child behind knowing how much they need you, how much you need them?" Her voice rose. Then fell. "That's what I carry around as one of the 'Unresolveds'."
A sadness radiated from her. A sadness so intense that he felt it draining the warmth from his body. He put his arms around her.

"Do you know how good it feels to hold your mum after all those years?"

"Do you know how good it feels to hold your child?"
God, this made 'Long Lost Families' look tame.
And, again, for that short time, the rest of the world really did cease to exist until, eventually, they let their arms fall back, tired but elated. Contentment that he had never really known before. Alongside a certain detached humour that another lover of the surreal would understand. This was, he thought, about as surreal as it got. Rene Magritte would have been delighted.
As they sat next to each other on the sofa, he suddenly felt drained. Not only that but he also noticed that his mother seemed to be as well. His first response to this was to panic.

"Mum, what's happening?"
She, too, looked frightened as if she wasn't sure. Then she remembered what she'd been told by the others. That the

first session, especially, would be extremely draining and that a symptom of this, tiredness on one part and a fading on the other, would herald the ending.

"Michael, don't worry, but I think that we may nearing the end of this meeting."

"No, it can't be. Not yet. We've only just started."

"It's OK. Just call me tomorrow and we'll carry on." Real panic set in.

"How do I know you'll be here?"

"Trust me, my child. I'm not letting you go now." With that the fading increased although the voice continued.
"Love you, Michael."

"Mum, please don't go. I need you."
That statement a first for him.
She seemed calmer than him (not a difficult state of affairs).
"Don't worry. I will be here tomorrow."
As they both stood up and hugged, he realised that his arms were empty. That she had, in fact, already gone.
"Fuck it. Fucking, fucking, fuck it." Words that he hoped she couldn't hear from wherever she was. Utterly drained he sat on the sofa and cried. It was as if she's died again. Only, this time, the adult knew what had happened. How would he keep going until tomorrow? With Gaynor and Ellie away, he was on his own and, indeed, he felt more alone than he ever had in his whole life.

The following day and, especially, the night were to prove one of the longest he'd ever lived through. He always hated the sleepless nights that he suffered occasionally, but this one was to prove to be the worst, by far. Eventually, in the early hours, he got up to read, an old standby. Two hours were to pass before physical tiredness was to catch up with his emotional side and he went back to bed. Just how long would he have to wait the following day before he could get in touch with his mother again?

Another Visit

He woke up to the sound of his mobile. It was Gaynor checking to see how he was. He was never very good at telephone conversations even with those he loved. With so much that he wanted to say and so little of the circumstances that he felt able to, especially at a distance, this was no exception. Eventually, she said, "Mike, you sound a bit distracted, Are you OK?"

"Of course, It's just that I miss you and Ellie." A white lie that he would put right when they got home.

"Us too. Will you pick us up at the station?"

"Yeah. Give me a call when you're getting into London. Love you."

"Love you too."
He heard the line go dead and decided that, now he was awake, he might as well get up. After a quick wash and a cup of tea, he sat in front of the computer, hoping that work might distract him. It didn't. Somehow he managed to get through the morning. It helped, of course, that he'd been

through difficult times before although this wasn't just difficult, it was nigh on impossible. However, he managed to control his emotions and not let them run free. Eventually, he could wait no longer and he called her name. It was late morning and there was no reply. Panic set in. How did he know that this would happen just when the dream of a lifetime had come true? Was everything about to come to a stop just as it had started? Right now, it appeared that it would. It was lunchtime after he'd called any number of times that she flickered into view.

"Mum", the relief was immense.

"Michael, I haven't got much time right now. I'm not strong enough. Can you call me when it gets dark with you. I think that should be enough time. Don't worry, I just need to get stronger."

And with that she was gone. Still concerned but, somewhat reassured, he decided that some fresh air would help. Thinking things through had long been a strong point for him and a walk would clear his head.

He came home as the evening was setting in and managed to wait a further hour or so. By which time it was dark. He couldn't wait any longer so, with some apprehension, to say the least, he called. He needn't have worried as she appeared clear and physical just as she had the day before.

"Mum, I was so worried that you wouldn't make it."

"So was I, only, in my case, worried about you being worried."

Another instance of his own way of thinking and with it, a pleasing affirmation of where he'd picked it up from. It was starting to appear that this person, who he had no memory of, may have had a greater impact on his life than he imagined. He felt good at the thought. He then realised that they were holding one another tightly and the naturalness of that was also a cause of immense pleasure.

"I know that this is your house, Michael, but can we please sit down as you're making me nervous?"

At which, they both smiled. And, of course, sat down.

"Are you OK, my child?"

"Well, the last 12 hours hasn't been a great deal of fun but you're here now. Perhaps I won't worry so much next time."

"I'm sorry but with everything else that was going on I forgot to warn you. It was only when I got back that one of the others asked me if I'd explained things to you and I had admit that I'd forgotten. They all laughed and told me that I'd probably not been the first to do that. Indeed, it was probably more likely than not. Still, I'm here now so, where were we? And it's my turn to ask questions. First of all, I'd like to know what you remember about those early days?"
He'd expected this question but rather hoped that she wouldn't have asked it again. Now he would have to tell her.
"Mum, I'm really sorry but I have hardly any memories of when we were together. Just the odd snippet. And none of your being ill or of you going away." It was funny how this arch rationalist couldn't bring himself to say the word.

"It's alright, Michael, you can say it. You mean when I died."
Unfortunately, her saying it didn't make it any easier for him. Not that it was frightening just that it made him feel uncomfortable. He was quiet for a minute or so as if his mind was trying to process the information for the first time. He felt her arm around his shoulder but, with that, his old discomfort and awkwardness; as if he'd never learned how to just be natural with another adult. It wasn't meant to be this way.
"Are you OK, my child?" A look of concern on her face.

"Mum, I thought that this would be perfectly natural and it has been but, for some reason, right now it doesn't feel that way. I don't want to be but I feel a little awkward with you holding me while we have this conversation."
She moved her arm away, a little too sharply for him.
"It's not that I don't want you to put your arm around me, it's just that I'm not used to it. Aunt Ada tried but she wasn't

you!" He reached out and held her hand. "Physical closeness was something that was largely missing from my life after you died and I think that we need to recreate it bit by bit. Is that OK?"

"You know it is." Something she said while not letting go of his hand and something that he understood to be the start of the process. She still didn't let go and he didn't push her away.

"Can you tell me what you do remember?"

"I remember the cherry tree in the back garden and the swing that Bob fixed up on it. I also remember laying on my stomach in the passage with the front door open when it was raining. The raindrops were splashing in the puddles and you said that they were soldiers, like my father. I remember you washing up at the sink and me asking you to play. You were wearing a brown skirt with dots on it. I also remember someone called Olive shutting me in the cupboard under the stairs and being outside the pub with other kids while the adults were inside. The footbridge over the railway. That's still there. And the canal, although that was filled in a long while ago. I went back there when I moved to London 30 years ago and the whole area has been replaced with blocks of flats although Silwood Street is still there."

"No memory of me putting you to bed or anything?"

"Sorry, Mum, no. I think when you died, I shut down. Bob did come round to take me home on Sundays but that stopped after a few weeks. From what I can gather, he was told that it was too upsetting for me. I didn't see Bob or any of the Hudsons until Doll got in touch nearly twenty years later."

"How could anyone do that? How dare they?" This, quietly, in a very angry voice. "Where was your father?"

"He went back to his unit and got married a few months later. He brought Eve home to see me then and left. I didn't hear from him until I was 14."

She looked at him is utter astonishment.
"How could he? What happened to you?"

"I was handed over to Aunt Ada and Uncle Bill. Doll told me that she was delegated to do it soon after the funeral. It's my first real memory, standing at the Colleen Bawn and then being taken away by Aunt Ada."
At that she just put her head in her hands aghast at what she'd just heard.
"I saw you and your father when I was laid out in the house and thought that you were with him. Couldn't you have stayed with Bob or Doll?"

"Apparently not. I understand that there was no love lost between the two families."

"Not all of them."
With that she reached out and held his hands as if her life depended on it. Not that he was complaining.
"Mum, it's OK. It was 70 years ago."

"Not for me it wasn't. I should have fought harder then, maybe,…….."

"Mum, it wasn't your fault. There wasn't anything you could have done. Anyway we're here together now with so much to talk about and me with the chance to make you proud."
Through her tears he heard "I always was".
"Yes but now I'll be able to feel it."
Words seemed unnecessary so there weren't any. Just two people content in each other's company and happy to be so. Eventually she broke the silence. "I knew there'd be a whole lifetime that I'd know nothing about but I never thought that it would have been like this. Especially after I think that I'd told him what I wanted".

"You mean that he was there before you died?"

"Not for long but yes. That's why I said "think" as I wasn't exactly aware of much of what was going on. I never expected this although, knowing your father, I'm not surprised."

"Aunt Doreen called him a moral coward. That seems a bit harsh although I know what she meant".

"Which was?"

"That, in personal situations, he tended to take the easy way out, was self centred and impulsive. The youngest brother to six older sisters who, probably, spoilt him."

"That sounds about right. A bit of a ladies' man with the gift of the gab."
She couldn't help but notice that this was a conversation that he didn't seem keen to continue.
"You didn't like your father?"

"It's a long story, Mum, and anyway, he's been dead for over 20 years. I didn't even go to the funeral."

"Michael, that's very sad."

"Not really. I couldn't be bothered and it was a long way to Taunton. Besides, I had work to do."

"Did you go to Doreen and Bill's?"

"Of course."

"Like I said, it's sad."

"Mum, I really would like to talk about us. Well, you, in fact. I'd like to get to know you not just as my mum. What was your life like?"

"Not that interesting really. I was born in 1912 and lived my whole life in the Islands. Just like your father's family, there were ten of us. Walter, Henry, Alice, Jim, Maud, Jack,

Doll, Len, Bob and me. My mum and dad were Jim and Alice. He was a slaughterman and a butcher and died from Farmers' Lung when I was 20. Walter's son was killed in the Docks and my sister, Lally, died young from the same weak heart that I had. I lived with my mum until your father and me got married. We never had much money but no one did in those days. Like Lally and a lot of other children, I got rheumatic fever and, years later, the doctor told me that that was what caused me to have a weak heart."

"That ties in with what Lal told me. That, when I was born, the doctor had told him that you'd be lucky to see my first birthday."

"Lal, that old bugger could never resist telling a good story. Still, in this case, it was probably true. Rheumatic fever and the weak heart."

"I know, I've got your death certificate where it's all listed. Doll also gave me some bits and pieces including the first photo of you I'd ever seen. That, a funeral card and my birth certificate. Holding the certificate that you'd used to register my birth, something you must also have held, was amazing. Very precious."

"You'd never seen one before?"

"No, like I said, you were never mentioned. It was as if you'd never existed. At least that's what I thought."

"Anyway, I met your dad because your Uncle Lal and my brother, Bob, both worked in the docks. Bob was on the floating timber. Your father was a right charmer and I fell in love with him. Unfortunately some of his family thought that mine were ne'er do wells and that I was far too old for him and mine thought that he was a womanizer who thought of lot of himself. Maybe there was some truth in all of those things."

"You really loved him, didn't you?"

69

"Of course. Until you came along he was my only sunshine. Until that letter."

"Yes, Aunt Doll told me what happened."

A deep sadness came into her eyes. "Dear Doll and Bob. Always there for me." He reached out and covered her hand with his.

"I'd like to be from now on."

"My little man. Again."

"Only not so little now."

"No and it's taking some getting used to. I see the adult in front of me and I hear his voice but, in my head, it's still Michael."

"Most people call me Mike but Michael seems right from you. Anyway, you and my father?"

"Well, we met before the war when your father was 18 and I was 22. It was a few years after my dad died. He lived with his parents in Nelldale Road and worked for his father in the coopering business under the arches. Bob and Daisy took me out for a drink one evening with Lal and Nora with your father in tow."

"Do you know if there were any times when the families met earlier?"

"I don't know of any. Why?"

"Well, I've done a lot of research into the family history. I even found a drawing of the house that my great grandparents moved into when they came over from Ireland, probably in the 1870's. It was Number 42 George Row."

"What's that got to do with my family then?"

"Well, I found out that your mum, Alice Colyer, once lived in the same house. I thought that, as she was born in

1881, maybe they'd moved in after the Daligans moved out or even lodged together for a while."

"I didn't know that but I wouldn't be surprised. Our world in the docks was quite a small one. So maybe there was a bit of history there. If not, it's quite a coincidence, don't you think?"

"It would seem so but, like you say, the world was a much smaller one than it is today as was that of my childhood. Anyway, you were saying?"

"Well, it didn't take long for Dorrie to ask me out and we had a couple of years together before the war broke out. Your father had always wanted to join the army although your grandfather wasn't too keen and neither was I. Still, he felt that it would give him a career instead of making barrels and, as soon as the war broke out, he joined up, in the Tank Corps. He was commissioned quite early and finished up as a Captain. Other than a few short periods of leave, we didn't see very much of each other after that. It was the same for all the women. Before the war, we walked out together, often in Southwark Park which had a bandstand as well as a Lido and a boating lake."

"Did you take me there?"

"Of course. All the women took their children. The new ones to show off and the others so that they could go on the swings or for a paddle in the water."
A large grin appeared on his face. "I used to go there after I went to live with Aunt Ada. Me, Michael and Richard. We played in the paddling pool with our small boats and went to the Lido and the swing park. I always wondered if you took me." He thought it best not to mention the Witch's Hat which he still had flashbacks about. "I went there with my youngest daughter when she was small and it was much as I'd remembered it. So, I took Ellie where you'd taken me!"
They both smiled at the thought until she said, "I'd loved to have done that with the two of you." Some minutes passed in silence until she said, "It's OK, my child, it was a long

71

time ago. "Anyway, we went to The Baron's Arms and The Europa, near Paradise Street where Lal and Nora lived. Often with Bob and Daisy, Doll and Freddy and Lal and Nora. Sometimes we'd go up west to see the lights and how the other half lived. When it was just the two of us, your father would take me to the pictures, The Star Cinema and The Rialto. One of the first films we saw was "The Private Life of Don Juan", quite appropriate I thought later. Looking back, they seemed like good times. We were both in work. Your father with his dad in the barrel making business and me at Peak Freans where some of your father's sisters worked. None of us ever went short of biscuits, that's for sure. Garibaldi were my favourites. Like most couples, we'd talked about getting married and having a family and then the war came along. Anyway, he joined up and I saw him occasionally while he was in training. We decided to get married anyway and we did at St James' Church. It was August 1940 and we had a couple of days together before Dorrie had to go back to his unit. The blitz started a few weeks after that."

"Doll gave me a photo of the wedding which I keep in my photograph album along with your marriage certificate and other bits and pieces."

"Would you mind if I saw them?"

"Of course not." This as he walked into the other room, returning with it under his arm. The next hour was spent doing another of those things that most families take for granted. Looking at old photos, albeit, ones that didn't include many of his mum or her family although, thankfully, did include Bob and Doll. A ghost and her son crying at a shared joy and sadness. It was then that he saw another shared characteristic; that of dealing with the emotion in order to get on with the business in hand.

"So where were we?" He heard her say.

"The onset of the war. That must have had quite an effect, then the blitz?"

The response was a long drawn out "Yes" followed by "I survived. At least for a while."

She smiled at the thought as did he at the darkness of her humour. It was good to discover what they had in common and where he got it from.

"So, what was it like?"

Sorry, Mum. That just came out.

"A bit unreal really. After all, it had only been 20 years since the Great War. I was too young to remember that much but I do remember my family talking about it when the men came home. They certainly didn't want another war. Nobody did. And, yes, we'd heard what Herr Hitler was doing but we thought that none of it would affect us. Especially after the Prime Minister came back waving his piece of paper. Even then, it was another year before war was declared. Your father, though, thought that Mr Churchill was right and that war was probably inevitable. It did cause arguments between us as I thought that he was looking for an excuse to join up."

"Yes, Uncle Bill told me that although granddad didn't want him to."

"Anyway, he enlisted as soon as he could. Not that it mattered as he'd have been called up anyway. I was angry and also very frightened but there was nothing any of us could do. It was very scary being caught up in, what your father called, the wheel of history. Looking back, it was probably the beginning of the end for us then. We'd had as much of our lives together as we ever would have. Mind you, we weren't alone in that."

She stopped, her eyes almost looking back at events that had occurred over 80 years ago. It seemed best not to interrupt her thoughts and he didn't. Eventually, he said, "I'm so sorry, Mum. It seems as though you never had much of a chance."

"The trouble with the future is that you don't know what it will bring and, in our case, it may have been best not to know. He wasn't a bad person you know, just a bit of a dreamer and, of course, a charmer. Not a great combination."

"And thoroughly spoilt."

"Maybe. Still, as they say, it's water under the bridge. Now, where was I?"

"Dad had just signed up?"

"Oh yes. Then we had the "Twilight War", what became known as the "Phoney War", before the real thing arrived on our doorstep. And, in the docks, it really was on our doorstep. They even set up anti aircraft guns in the park. Can you imagine that? Guns where your children played. We knew then that this war would be different. It wouldn't be fought just by men across the Channel but by all of us, at home. Women and children would die. Then it really started."

"Mum, are you alright with this?"
She smiled, "I am now, my child. I wasn't at the time. None of us were. You like your history, don't you?"

"How can you not and, anyway, this is real history, where it happened from someone who lived through it. The only people who talked to me about it before was Uncle Bill when he described what it was like fighting in Europe and my father who described the aftermath. Until I spoke to Bill, when I was in my mid twenties, I never realised what a close run thing it was."

"I remember the day that it started. It was a Sunday soon after we got married and Dorrie had returned to his unit. The sun was shining then, in the afternoon, the sirens sounded and we got under the stairs. I was petrified. Then you could hear the bombers overhead and the guns opening up. The bombs were the worst as you could hear the explosions and feel the ground shaking. I thought that we would die. We all did. It seemed to go on for hours and then we heard the planes returning home. We'd survived. Except

74

that it wasn't over. They came back that evening and the bombs dropped again, until the early hours. We thought that it would never end. We certainly never imagined that it would go on for another two months, night after night. Or that the war would continue for another five years!"

Silwood Street, Oldfield Grove, Landmann's Way and Reculver Road, they all got bombed. Your Aunt Ada and her husband were bombed out of their house in Henwood Road, just by the park. Some of my friends' children died. I don't think they ever got over it. You can't imagine how scared we were. It didn't go away but, somehow, we learned to live with it. After all, we never knew whether or not we'd still be alive the following day. In fact, that's one of the reasons why your father and me got married when we did. There seemed no reason not to and we might as well make the best of things while we had the chance."

All the time we just felt exhausted, hungry and very, very frightened. Can you imagine trying to live your life while not knowing whether you would be alive or dead in the morning? And that your death would be violent? Seeing your neighbours killed? Being frightened to go out, but knowing that staying in wouldn't make much difference? There was nowhere that was safe. What was worse was seeing my mum beside herself with worry without her husband to be there for her and knowing that I couldn't do anything about it."

She stopped and, for a brief moment, it really was September 1940 and they were in Edale Road.

"Mum, you really don't have to do this. I feel like I'm getting you to talk about things that have just happened."

"Michael, to me it's as if it was recently. You have to remember that I died just two years after the war was over. It is fresh to me and it helps to talk about it."

She stopped and it was obvious that even the retelling hadn't lessened the impact much.

How could he have been so bloody stupid?

He reached out for her hand. "I'm sorry, Mum, I didn't think."

"Why should you, it happened before you were born?

Anyway, we got through it and that's the main thing. Because we did, you were born."

"And the rest, as they say, is history."
He was getting to know this woman and, in the process, learning more about her than he might have done in more conventional circumstances. So, every cloud could have a silver lining after all.

"So, my child, shall I continue?"

"Do you really want to?"

"Just to tell you about your father and me and how you came about."

"Mum, I think I know that."
She smiled. "No doubt you do, my child, no doubt you do."

"Unfortunately, we didn't get much official information about those who were fighting although I knew that he'd got commissioned and that the Tank Corps were in North Africa. With the married allowance I got, I managed to get a small place opposite my mum's in Edale Road. Then, in September 1941, Dorrie managed to get a short leave from Egypt. I don't know how he did it but, then, he always did have the gift of the gab. You were born the following summer. So we had some time to ourselves and, soon after he left, I found that I was in the family way. He came home again when his mum died and that was the only time that the three of us were ever together. In the spring of 1943. I never saw him again."
Her mouth tightened at that. So, there was bitterness, after all.

"Yes, I have the photo. It looks like it's been torn in two and then pasted back together again."
Silence between the two of them. His mum still angry at what had happened and him angry at what had made her angry.
Finally, he said, "He stayed in the army after the war and finished up as a Major."

"Did he now? He was a Lieutenant when I last saw him.

Anyway, one morning that letter arrived where he said that he wanted a divorce to marry that woman. From the Robinson's Barley Water family wasn't it? It must have been in the autumn of 1947 and I was already ill. That was the last straw."

"So from cooper to Major, marrying into the society that he'd always hankered after."

"They did get married, then?"

"Yes, in March 1948."

"Oh, he didn't waste any time, did he?"
The implication was obvious.

"Did they have a family?"

"Two boys, Phillip in 1949 and Simon two years later." He thought that that was the best way to respond. She appeared to brush off the thought of any further questions preferring to stick to her own life; something that he preferred anyway.

"Apart from the fact that the letter came out of the blue, no one in our family had ever been divorced. I felt as if I'd failed and I had you to consider. Also, a divorce meant that I wouldn't get any allowance from your father. That meant that we wouldn't be able to pay the rent and buy food. I was at my wit's end as I thought that you'd be taken away from me. . Bob and Doll said that they'd help out but they had no money and families of their own. All I could think of was wanting your father home with us so that we could be a family and that that wasn't ever going to happen. I just couldn't keep going. I'm so sorry."
As she said this, she looked at the floor. He thought it best not to mention the nurse in South Africa that he'd been told about or the implied threat to Ada that, if she didn't take him, the other option was in a home for boys. Anyway, it had been the biggest war in history when any normal

standards of behavior probably went out of the window. They both reached out to hold one another, both of them sad at what had happened and, by implication, what might have been. After a minute or so, they pulled apart and smiled at one another.

"We are a pair of softies, aren't we?"

"Maybe we are, Mum, in which case the world could do with a lot more of them. Now, do you mind if I make a cup of tea?"

"Of course, my child. You look as though you need one."

"So do you."

"I'm OK but I do need a breather too."
As he waited for the kettle to boil, he started to realise that, much as he'd dreamt of this happening all his life, he hadn't ever thought it through. There was certainly more unhappiness unearthed in getting to be happy although it was certainly worth it. He sat down and put his cup on the table feeling awkward again. Yes she was a ghost but could he do nothing to ease any of this as a simple cup of tea was doing for him?

"Mum, I know you don't need sustenance, but is there nothing I can do. I feel that I'm making it worse."
She laughed. "Michael, I've waited for a long time for this and, I'm really fine. My emotions are being sustained by you and they keep me here. Let's keep going, please?"
He beamed. "Of course. I was just worried about you."

"No need."

"I did try, you know. When he got his commission, I asked Lal if he knew any books that would help me understand how to behave and speak properly. He did his best but I don't think either of us were under any illusions. I was from Mud Island and your father was now in the Officers' Mess. I don't think that I had much of a chance."

"You and me both, Mum. When he came back from

Malaya, as it was then, with his new family, he came to Doreen and Bill's to ask me to go and live with them. Once he'd heard me speak, he arranged for me to have elocution lessons. So we both tried and neither of us had much luck, it would seem."

"When he came back from Malaya?"

"Yes, he was posted there after Germany before he eventually came back to England in 1956. That's when he wrote to Aunt Doreen and I went to live with them. I'll tell you about that when it's my turn. So what happened next?"

"Unfortunately, I'm not too sure. I wasn't in a fit state to do anything and Bob and Doll looked after you when I wasn't able to, which was most of the time. They must have tried to shield you from what was happening but it must have been almost impossible. Anyway, it wasn't long afterwards that I gave up the ghost." She smiled at the unintended joke as did he. "From then on, for a while it was all very hazy."

"Mum, are you OK?"

"Michael, like I said, I've had a whole lifetime to get used to it. So, please ask away. It's OK."
He plucked up courage and asked, "What happened when you died?"

"To be honest, I wasn't really conscious towards the end. I remember you coming in to see me and then I just drifted away. It was pretty frightening although it was also a relief to be free from all that I'd had to put up with over the months. The problem was that I had no idea what would happen. I hoped for pearly gates but dreaded that it might be the opposite. It took me a while to realise that there weren't either. I do remember still being angry with your father for what he'd done, but it was too late by then. I also remember looking down on all of those in the front room and feeling very sad. They had most of their lives in front of them and

79

I didn't. I didn't want to die and leave you but the pain had been pretty constant. I couldn't bear the thought of leaving you but I had nothing left in me. I was exhausted."

Her voice dropped as she said this, remembering almost as if it was yesterday. Also overcome with the enormity of what had happened, he reached out and held her hands in his. The holding becoming an embrace with mother and son alone with each other in a closeness he'd dreamt of for as long as he could remember.

"It's OK, Mum. We're together now. Just you and me." She smiled at that thought as they both relished the moment. If there was a heaven, this was about as close as it got for both of them.

"So you knew that you were dead?"

"I think so. Like I said, scared, worried and not able to get back to where I'd been. It's something that I prefer not to think about too much."

"Of course. Sorry. As I got older, I always thought that you'd given up and left me until a friend said that fighting for all that time didn't demonstrate someone who hadn't tried. I'd never seen it that way. I'm sorry, mum. I should have thought."

"You've no need to apologise. You were a child, Michael. Can you imagine that happening to any of my grandchildren?"

"My worst nightmare other than them dying first." As he thought about what a lovely way that was to describe them.

"You shouldn't blame your father, you know."
His lips fixed themselves shut.

"I was the one who made much of the running. You know the age difference between us and I didn't want to be left on the shelf. He was quite a catch, you know."
Again no words.

"I'm sorry, mum, but I think Aunt Doreen got it right. All I can think of is a man who kept coming back into my life just to mess it up before leaving again. Not once but every time. Why would anyone do that? Did you know that he told Ada that it was either her or a home for boys?" There he'd said it. "He didn't need to do that as Ada would never have said no anyway. And to leave me with Uncle Bill when everyone knew how strict he was."

"I'm sorry, Michael. I can't defend him for that."

"It wasn't your fault. It was his and I can't forgive him. If you ever see him, you can pass my message on."

"I don't, anyway, I don't even know where he's buried but I suspect that it's too far away for me to be able to make any contact. It's not like a big holiday camp reunion here, you know."
At that he smiled at the memory of all the holiday camps he'd been to as a child; the wooden huts, the fancy dress competitions, the forfeits for being late for meals and, "Goodnight, Campers" being sung at the end of the day.
"I wanted you to grow up as my son."

"I'm sorry but I grew up as a Daligan and saw myself as one. Funny that you were the important one who I missed yet I always saw you as the Lou Hudson that you were; not the Lou Daligan that you became when you got married."

"Maybe because I had hardly any married life at all. None of us did. We just had our families around us as we'd always had. I might as well have been single. Now, please tell me about yourself."

"It's funny but I thought you'd know it all."

"Michael, people may think of us as supernatural but we don't have supernatural powers. I have my memories but not yours. Plus, of course, the knowledge of those other 'Unresolveds' that I talk to."

"Wow, where to start? How long have you got?"

81

"I'm not sure but, from talking to the others, I know that it's the strength of our feelings that gets me here and lets me stay. Although it seems that I have to go back behind the veil to allow both of us to recoup enough to enable me to come back."

"Just a minute." he said and went into the spare room. He came back with a grin on his face and four books in his hands. Handing over one of them he said "You could just read this. It's called 'The Other Side of the Doors' and it's my life story."

"You've written all those. My son, an author." The pride shone in her eyes and the joy at that was reflected in his.

"Could you read it to me? I'd like that. I don't want to sit here reading and we can't take objects from one realm into the other."

"Of course." And with that he turned to page 11, the Dedication. At the mention of her name she looked at him with a smile of surprise and delight on her face. She also, he noticed, had tears in her eyes.

"Thank you for that, Michael."

"My pleasure, Mum."
Then he turned the page to 'Michael's Story.' "Mum, this bit is sad but don't worry it gets better the more I read." So he did, from his time with Ada and Bill, his rescue by Doreen and Bill, their wish to adopt him, his father returning 9 years after her death to promptly sign him into the army at 15 and then his first, unhappy, marriage. Perhaps being dead gave her great patience but she listened without interruption although not without emotion. Maybe it was the story or maybe it was that understanding and intuition that he'd always been brought up to believe that mothers had, in a way that fathers didn't.
"I think that's as good a spot as any to finish for now, especially as my throat is dry."

"It does get better, Michael, doesn't it?"

"Yes, Mum, it does although it has its moments along the way. The important thing is to look at where I am now. The way things have turned out in the long run. Perhaps if I'd known that, I'd have worried less and done more."

"More what?"

"Just doing my bit in the world as well as getting recognised for my writing."

"Fingers crossed for you, my child."
It was then that he felt the tiredness hit him and noticed that his mother's figure was starting to fade. For an instant she looked frightened as she, too, realised what was happening. How could she not? It was happening to her.

"Michael, I'm sorry but I think we're coming to the end for now."
Despite himself, he felt that awful feeling in his stomach that he had when one of his relationships ended. Even though, this time, he now knew that she'd be back.
He reached out to take her hand. Just in time. "See you tomorrow. Same time."
Then she was gone and he felt drained. The deep emotional draining that he felt after a particularly intense therapy session. In this case, a marathon one.

The cup of tea that followed was as refreshing as any he'd ever tasted and, boy, would he have something to tell Gaynor and Ellie when they got home. He put the cup down and sat on the sofa, to be woken up by the sound of the doorbell. Just a delivery. A parcel for Ellie from the real world. Something that reminded him, a lover of the surreal, of just how weird this all was and how quickly he'd become used to it. Roll on tomorrow.

He Needn't Have Worried

As always when his family were away, he didn't sleep well. Waking at 7, he got up to his usual tea and toast. Normal. An early morning run along the canal followed by a shower, also normal. Get his copy of The Guardian and read it over coffee. Still normal. Quick crossword, again normal. Write something, still normal. Yet what he needed was a return to the surreal world that he'd experienced over the past few days. Fortunately (although it didn't seem so at the time) he'd experienced enough relationship breakdowns to know what it was like to have to sit waiting with that feeling of apprehension. The experience now served him in good stead.

Impatient to call he may have been, but he fought the impulse. His early life had given him the need to control as much as possible, knowing that events would always conspire. Masochism was also a trait as was the idea that you should get your retaliation in first even if you were its only target. Anyway he didn't want to disturb his mum. Funny idea he thought, disturbing the dead? So, he thought he'd write it all down. That way he would have a reasonably factual record of what had happened. Who knew, it might become another book? Lunchtime passed and it was into the afternoon when, on her last visit, she'd told him that that was better. Surely she would be rejuvenated by now?

"Mum, are you there?" He needn't have worried. The same person stood in front of him wearing the same clothes with the same smile on her face.

"Michael, I was getting worried."

"I tried to give you as much time as possible as I thought that that would make you stronger."

"Well, it seems to be working OK so, perhaps, we can both stop worrying so much. Please, give me a hug."
Why had he needed to be reminded of that when it should have been automatic? That panic of being left alone all those years ago and, as a result, not letting anyone in. Even his mother? You idiot. Just get over yourself.

"The others did tell me not to worry, that it would happen. But as it had drained me so much after the first time, I couldn't help but not do so."

"Still you're here now so can I have a hug too?"
It's what he wanted to do even as he felt uncomfortable doing it and, yes, he had to get over whatever it was that was making him feel this way. This was his mother, for God's sake. So he held her until, a little awkwardly, he stepped back and they both sat down.

"How are you?" she asked.

"I should feel ecstatic and I think I do. It's just that it's very strange and I need to get used to it. I want being with you to be the most natural thing in the world and, somehow, it's not. It's as if I need to get used to it. Daft really."

"Perhaps not so daft, Michael. Maybe we just need to do

what we feel like doing, after all it's what children and parents do. Except in our case where I was torn away from you so that we never grew up together."

"Yes, it's something I talked to Dan Twomey about. Unlike other people, we never got beyond that mother and child stage and, as a result, I never experienced life with you with all its trials and tribulations. I never thought that we'd get the chance to talk about it."

"There are stranger things in heaven and earth."

"Aunt Doreen used to say that. OK, so, let's just talk and get to know one another even if it will be like trying to compress a whole lifetime into the short time we've got.

"OK, my child, then you can read me some more so that I can get to know you better."
Maybe you get to be natural by just doing it and less with thinking about it. Hadn't other people told him that in the past? What they didn't know was that being natural with children was easy. It was adults that were the problem. Still, he had to learn sooner or later.

"One thing, though, Mum, how much of the modern world do you know about?"

"Well, I didn't know much during the time the cemetery was closed as we'd had no newbies to tell us what was happening and no visitors who we could pick up snippets from. But, it's better now. I'm not sure that I'd like it as it sounds like there's a great deal of hustle and bustle. Too much that's seen as immediate when it really isn't and little of the closeness that we had in my day".

"I'd say that that was true although I wouldn't turn the clock back, I would be a bit more choosy about some of the technology created. It seems to put people in touch with one another more but I feel that it can close them off from the real world. You can't beat what we're doing now by being with one another just talking."

"But you said that you like your own company."

"I do it's still good to have other people around. Aren't you ever lonely?"
"Not during my "resting" times. Much of the time, that is."

"And the rest?"

"Not so much lonely, as I have others I can speak to. We're all a bit wistful and regretful, though, for what we've missed."

"Just like being alive, really."

"Yes, I suppose so, except for those last few weeks. With you and the sickness, I had my hands full. Towards the end, is wasn't good, that's for sure."

"I'm sorry."

"Michael, none of it was your fault."

"I felt as though it was. I remember you being very upset and I thought that I was to blame. If I hadn't done this or that, you would be fine. Even now I play a game in my head; that everything will be alright if I can get to that next crack in the pavement before a car goes by."

"We all have our ways of coping and you were a real help to me. For so long you gave me the strength to carry on. Your father's letter though......."
She trailed off as if she were reliving the occasion. He reached out and touched her hand.

"It was a long time ago, mum, and he certainly got his comeuppance in the end."

"What do you mean?"

"Well, I don't think that he and Eve were very happy. I doubt that she got what she'd expected. The war affected him greatly and he wasn't the same person afterwards. And, even without that, there's a big difference between the social life of any army officer and his wife and making a marriage work, day to day. Anyway, they retired him ten years later in that way that the army disposes of those it no longer needs. For a while he had the status that he wanted but I don't think he was happy. I think Eve had expectations which took a nosedive even before he left the army and I doubt that being the wife of the village shopkeeper was on her agenda any more than it was on his. And that's where they finished up. Even before the mobile home. As I mentioned yesterday, after the "fight of the geriatrics" he wrote to Lal saying that it would be best if they didn't get in touch with him again and considered him dead. The last time I saw him was at my Aunt Thora's 80th when Ellie was a baby. That was the first time since Simon's wedding 20 years earlier. Surrounded by his sisters, he was in his element. I remember looking at him. He was holding hands with Thora and Eileen, laughing, his eyes shining, and I thought "Why did you stay away from all this?" I didn't even go to his funeral. Anyway, enough of him. I'm interested in us, now." She tried not to show it but he couldn't help but notice how sad she was. "You were my child, my little boy and, like any mother, I ploughed everything into you. Until I got too weak. Do you have no memory of me? Of any of it?"

"Not really although I recently read that a child's memory doesn't usually start until the age of 3 and you died when I was 5. I remember laying in the passage and watching raindrops splash into a puddle. You called them soldiers, like my father. The swing in the garden and the bridge over the railway but that's about it. The houses were pulled down in the 1960's and replaced with a big estate. I went back when I moved back to London in 1986. The canal is filled in but the bridge over the railway is still there. So is the Baron's Arms, although it's now flats."

"You have no memory of me at all?"

"I'm sorry but no, nothing."

She looked down for more time than he felt comfortable with and, again, he reached out. This time to be her comfort.
"I suppose I thought that the five years we had together would have left something to remember me by. That's hard to take, Michael."

He wished that he'd told a white lie. Then he remembered that little boy inside who would have seen the world through a child's eyes. Hence his blunt response.
"We're here now, mum. You and me, both adults and glad to be together. I wish the past had been other than as it was but this has been worth the wait. No one else in the world. Just you and me. Not something that I ever imagined. I love you."
OMG he'd said it.

"I love you too, Michael."
Enormous smiles all round and the comfort of each others' physical presence
"You know that I saw you when you visited my grave? I wanted to talk to you then but you were completely closed off. You came on a number of occasions with different people. A couple of times with Gaynor and Ellie, although she was growing up then."

"Yes, the three of us did go a few times as we did with Gaynor's mum and dad. That was just to show them around the cemetery. At that time, it was being cleared and tidied up. What they call "managed decay". However, it was in 1985 when I went for the first time to try to find where you were buried. Doll had given me some information and I went with my partner at the time, but the area was so overgrown that it was difficult. It was nearly another 30 years before I actually found the grave."

"Yes, I remember that too."

"It was one of the most amazing moments of my life. I felt completely at peace knowing that you were just six feet away. Unfortunately all of it was below my feet."

If she could use black humour, so could he. They both smiled broadly as she replied, "I know, I felt that too and knowing that you were just above where I lay gave me that feeling of RIP that we're supposed to have. I knew that, once you'd found me, you'd be back as you have been."

"I need to put a headstone, Mum. I want people to know where you are and that you did live."

"Thank you, my child. That would be very nice. As would reading me some more about your life. Do you mind?"

As he went to collect the book, walking back into the sitting room, he felt ten feet tall.

"So, where were we?"

"I think your father had just returned."

"Yes, he had. Mum, please let me know if it gets a bit much and I can skip parts if you need me to."

"Not so far, Michael and, hopefully, not at all. I want to know as much about you as possible, so let's see how we get on."

Eventually, he got to the part where his son was born and it was his feeling tired of reading rather than his mother tired of listening that brought him to a stop. That and, he noticed, her growing transparency.

"Mum, I think we need to call it a day."

"It would seem so." This with a great deal of reluctance on both their parts.

"See you tomorrow?"

"Of course. Same time."

"Love you, Michael." And, with that, she was gone just as he was reaching out to hold her. He hadn't realised that it could happen as quickly. All sorts of emotions went through him. Pleasure that they had met again and that it was as easy as he'd hoped that it would be. Supposing they hadn't got on well together? Real pleasure that he was able to talk to her without the stiltedness that he felt in some of his other relationships. All this sustained by the thought that that he would see her again, but for how long? He must remember to ask her that when they next met. Anyway he'd worry about that later. Then there was the sadness and emptiness that she'd left. That, he knew, would always be a problem for him, just like it would be for anyone else, only more so. Stop, he told himself, stop thinking. Perhaps some supper and a glass or two of wine would help. Along with a phone call that would skirt around what was happening. How the hell could anyone describe, even to their nearest and dearest, what had happened other than in person? Even face to face, it would sound pretty weird.

Settled in front of the television, he really didn't want to watch anything very taxing (not a problem these days) and flipped through the channels. He caught a rerun of "Vera". It also featured dead bodies. A couple of hours later, with more wine drunk than he'd realised, he staggered to bed. Even then, his sleep was full of vivid dreams, each of them involving his mother and his father, separately. Not usually one to think too deeply about the dreams, he had to acknowledge that the symbolism was of interest.

Getting to Know One Another Better

When he woke up, he still felt tired, as if he'd had a badly disturbed night which, you could say he'd actually had. Needing to clear his head, he decided that this afternoon's run would be better taken this morning. Not just for the exercise but also for the fact that the steady, repetitious monotony of pace would allow his mind to wander. He thought of it as a form of meditation and it worked for him. Collect his paper on the way home and then in the door to a shower, toast and milky coffee and a read of the latest news. It was rarely good these days and he didn't expect it to get any better.

The morning's routine over, he settled himself in front of the computer to write trying to keep the emotional pull at bay. Not just to give his mother time to recover but also for his own emotional equilibrium. Knowing that this wouldn't be a long term relationship, he needed to feel that he would be able to cope with the ending that he knew must come.

This denying himself her presence, at least for a while, was an essential part of that process. So he reasoned.

Lunchtime passed along with the phone call to Gaynor and Ellie to arrange to pick them up from St Pancras in the morning until, at last, he could surrender to the demands in his heart and call her. He saw no reason to believe that she wouldn't turn up but that didn't prevent him from being apprehensive. He should have had more faith. No sooner than he had sat down to call her than she appeared, smiling as much as he was.

"Hello, mum. You OK?"

"Why wouldn't I be? I may be dead but I feel more alive than I've done since I first met your father. How about you?" He smiled. "Not bad for someone who's been spending the last few days talking to a ghost."
She smiled back at the thought. "Or, in my case, talking to the living."

"Can I ask you something?"

"You know you can."

"Have many others that you know done this?"

"Well, I knew them while they were doing it but, as they became resolved, they said their goodbyes and left. We never saw them again. So, I know a lot about the procedure but none of us know what happens after. We assume that we just cease to exist."

"But you don't know for definite?"

"No, we don't. Like most families and friends, we talk to each other about our experiences when we're together so there is a sort of store of knowledge that we all learn from."

"So there must always be enough of you around at any one time to be able to do that."

"I suppose so. Are you always so inquisitive?"
He burst out laughing."Doreen used to say that I had a mind like a sponge. That I soaked up information."

"So you do get something from your father. In addition to your nose, that is?"

"Is there nothing of you in me?"

"I hope so although it's always difficult to see yourself in your children, isn't it?"

"Gaynor says that to me, although I can see some likeness of me in my own children and she and Ellie are very alike."

"The other thing that I wanted to know is how long have we got?"
Straight talking was something that he seemed to have got from his mother. A point he thought worthy of mention. Her response was immediate.
"When I realised how ill I was and that I wouldn't have the long life I'd hoped for, I think I must have felt that there wasn't as much time for the niceties. Then again, I could be fairly blunt at times, unlike your father."

"So, how long?

"As long as it takes, I hope?" He noticed that, in this case, she might have found a direct answer to be a little problematic.

"How about the rest of my life?"

"I'm sorry, Michael but that won't be possible. I've talked to the others and the consensus seems to be about a week or so . It depends on how quickly I get resolved but not too long, I fear."
It wasn't what he wanted to hear and, from her expression, it also wasn't what she wanted to tell him.
"How will you know?"

"It seems that it will get harder to maintain the contact we have and that we'll know when we can't do it anymore." He sensed that that was all that he was going to find out just now.

"It's funny but, when I first started seeing a therapist, one of the questions I asked him was how would I know when I was ready to call it a day. He told me that it was when I felt that I could live my life without too much hindrance from my past. At the time, I thought that was a bit of a copout but it proved to be right. So I guess we'll see, but best not to count on too long?"

"No, best not to."
It was something that neither of them wanted to dwell on. At least not right now.
"In the meantime, perhaps it's best if we try to think of it as being just friends visiting one another."

"I don't have that many friends and few that I visit. In fact I prefer my home and my own company. I have my family and just a few close friends and I like that but I'm not a great socialiser. I do like people but more as individuals than as a whole. Someone once said that the problem was that people complicate things and I kind of agree with that." Intuitively, she replied, "They don't mean to let you down and hurt you, you know."

"I know but often they do."
Idiot, why did you say that? It wasn't her fault!

"Michael, I'm here so, please, be quiet."
She looked at him, "Are you OK?"

"Yeah, why not?" He smiled at the realisation of an understanding of him as a person that came from being, well, just his mother. That felt good.

"What are you smiling about?"

"Just you being you and understanding."

"Michael, I may have been dead for years but I'll always be your mother."
He smiled even more. "I know and I'll always be your son."
She pushed his shoulder away as she said, "You silly bugger."
Being playful with other adults wasn't something he was used to so, another first. He was getting to like this person and the care and occasional spikiness in her responses. Maybe something that Dan Twomey had told him years ago that was missing in his life, that gradual growing older alongside your parents and getting to see them as adults with all their faults, was starting to happen. He hoped that they had enough time for all this as he was starting to enjoy it.
Better late than never, Mike.
Yes, I know. I don't need you to tell me.
"What were you thinking about?" she asked.

"Just something that Aunt Doreen would have said."

"You loved her, didn't you?"

"Not at the time but I've grown to realise that I did. Her and Uncle Bill rescued me."

Quietly this time "I'm sorry that they had to."

"Mum, as Dan once told me you mustn't beat yourself up, you did the best you could at the time. We're here now and the past is just that, the past. OK?"

"I'll try."

"So will I."
It was amazing that, in such a short space of time since their first meeting, he'd managed to break one of the habits of a lifetime. That of trying to make sure that relationships with your close family and especially the other relationships that he'd had, had to be perfect all the time. There could be no

cross words, no disagreements. As long, of course, that things were done in his way. He loved this person so had to like her, didn't he? The thought that he might upset her was a difficult one for him to accommodate, yet here he was accommodating it. This, set against the knowledge that this situation was temporary. It wouldn't last very long. Seventy years of waiting and mere days of being together. That was hard to take but, as Doreen would have said, "It is what it is." Was there anything that she didn't have a mantra for?

"Michael?"

"Sorry, Mum, I was miles away."

"I could see that."

"Mum, I know that this might seem like a silly question but, how did you feel about me?"

"Like any mother with a child. I loved you. You were my life, until it was all taken away." More sadness than bitterness, although of a depth beyond his experience.

"Did you not know that, Michael?"

"Well, I do now that we've been together and it's a bit overwhelming. But you died when I was a small child and I don't think I ever got to the stage where I realised those feelings for what they were. I guess I knew you loved my father because I must have heard you talk to Bob and Doll about it. You used to sing "My only sunshine" when you were unhappy."

"That was after he asked for a divorce. You remember that?"
He smiled sadly, "Yes, I do."
"What made you think that it was about Dorrie and not you?"

"Because you used to sing, "Please don't take my sunshine away" and I was still there."

"I really should have thought more but I was at my wit's end." Her voice trailed off.

He reached out and held her hand just as he'd tried to do as a child.

"What did you expect "your little man" to do, Mum? I just wanted you to smile."

She reached out and pulled her towards him, holding him tightly. It might have been a very, very long wait but, at last, that togetherness between this mother and her child, was as complete as it could ever be. The tears from both of them were cathartic as they just held one another. Finally, as they parted, she said,

"I'm here now and you really are my only sunshine."

"Time for a little read?" he asked, picking up the book.

"That would be nice. Where were we?"

"My son, Matthew, had just been born and I was about to leave the army."

"Rather as I'd hoped would happen to your father and me when the war ended. What is it they say about the sins of the fathers being visited on the sons?"

"You know, it's funny but, when I left, I'd been in the forces for almost half my life and I had no idea what awaited me. In fact, I was told by others that I wouldn't make it; that I'd be back. After all, hadn't they tried it and it hadn't worked for them. I remember telling one of them that he should watch my lips, "I won't be back" and I wasn't. The thought never occurred to me."

"Was it difficult then?"

"Not really, after all, I'd had quite a bit of experience by then. Mind you, I was lucky. Still, I'm jumping the gun and you'll find out what happened very soon."

"I'm all ears."

So, having got himself a glass of water and made himself comfortable, he opened the book at the bookmark and continued. This had become a pleasure that he'd never envisaged. An hour later, at the point where he'd divorced and started as new life, he ran out of steam. By the look of things, his mother too was tired.

"Does it get better, Michael? I think I need some good news at some stage."

"Well, it still has its ups and down but, in retrospect this point was where I started to get my life onto the track that I wanted it to be on. Not that I saw it that way at the time. It was just another step along the way. The difference was that, with custody of Tracey and Matt, I could just be me and that made all the difference. Perhaps that's why "The Road Not Taken" is my favourite poem."

"Two roads diverged in a yellow wood
And sorry that I could not travel both
And be one traveller, long I stood
And looked down one as far as I could
To where it bent in the undergrowth."

He looked up in surprise as she stopped reciting. "It was one of your father's favourites too. He used to read me poetry when we first met and nobody else had ever done that."

"Yes, he gave me "The Rubaiyat of Omar Khayyam" when I went to live with him and Eve. I remember him reading a verse about "a jug of wine and loaf of bread and thou beside me in the wilderness"

"And wilderness was paradise enow." He used to read it to me too."

"Do you think that he had regrets?"
"It would be nice to think so but I'm not sure. It always seemed to me that he wanted to get somewhere and that the future was more important to him than the past."

"I had that for a years until I realised that my past played a big hand in my future and that I was trying to shut that past out. In fact I managed to do just that but that didn't mean that it hadn't happened. And before you say anything, Mum, you couldn't stop your heart being weak."

It was then that a thought occurred to him. *"You idiot, why hadn't you thought about that before. She'd watched her sister Alice die from the same thing and pretty much knew that it might well happen to her and when. Christ almighty, why didn't you bloody think, Daligan?"*

At which point, he thought that it was best to change the subject. And quickly.

"Mum, now that I know that we haven't got very long, I need to ask you something."

"OK."

"Well, I can't get you up to Tracey and Matt and there might not be time to get them down here so, would you like to meet Gaynor and Ellie? They're due back tomorrow."

She smiled, "My, you're just like your father with your surprises aren't you? Although at least yours are pleasant ones. And, yes, I'd love to. I hope they'll like me."

"Don't worry they will. In that case, are you OK if I just read a little more as I'd like to jump to the chapters on my life since I met Gaynor so that you know something about her and Ellie. Do you mind?"

"Of course not. Off you go."

Half an hour or so later and his throat really was dry. Fortunately, he's reached a point at which he could stop as he noticed that she was starting to become lethargic.

"Sorry, Michael, I must go. Call me later when you're ready? Love you."

And, before he had the chance to say anything other than "Yes" and "Love you too", she was gone. At least he didn't get the chance to feel so anxious or maybe he was getting used to people that he loved leaving. And about time too. Now to telephone his wife and youngest daughter to make sure that nothing was amiss at their end and that they would be getting into St Pancras on time. But, what would he tell Gaynor and Ellie when he saw them? Yet, really, he knew the answer to that question. He would just sit them down and tell them what had happened. Just like he always did.

A Family Gathering

Three hours later and his difficulty in waiting for anything, even a bus, manifested itself. This, combined with his need to always double check everything made the situation worse. So, he called.

"Mum, can I talk to you, please?"

She came through straight away, looking worried.

"Michael, what's wrong?"

"Nothing, Mum. I just wanted to be sure. Are you still OK with this?"

"Why wouldn't I be?"

He laughed. "I have a bad habit of always checking to make sure that everything's alright. Talk to Ellie and Gaynor and they'll tell you."

"Well, I will soon and, yes, of course I'm OK. I've talked to some of the others and they're really pleased for me. Also, I think, a little bit envious."

"Because it hasn't happened for them?"

"Mainly, although there are stories of where it didn't go as well as people had hoped. Just like the families that they were part of when they were alive. You may always love them but that doesn't mean that you always like them."

"Gaynor tells me that I don't understand it and I don't. Yet, I do recognize it in my own life. One of the many contradictions I live with."

"Don't we all? Michael, much as I'd love to stay and talk to you, we're using valuable effort when we'll need it even more than usual when we meet."

"Why's that?"

"Well, it seems to be something to do with the fact that it takes more out of you and me if there is someone present not related by blood."

"Why should that be?"

"I don't know but I was talking to the others about it when you called."

"They seem to think that it's not blood but that blood ties are emotional ones. Well mostly. Meeting a stranger, as it does for the rest of you, means extra effort; at least for the first few times. Then, if you like them, it's easier."

"And if you don't?"

"When I was alive, I avoided those that I didn't like, except when they were, say, one of my brother's or sister's families. Then I made the effort. Fortunately, that effort didn't have repercussions for me staying around. Anyway, my child, I need to get back so that I can get myself ready. Love you."

"You too, Mum."
And, with that and a smile, she was gone. He just had time

to make himself a milky coffee when the phone rang. The train was about twenty minutes away and could he wait for them in the usual place behind St Pancras Station? Ten minutes later and he was sat in the car looking towards the back of the station. There they were, smiling as they saw him. Now to tell them.

They got home and, while they unpacked, he put the kettle on. Tea for Ellie and strong coffee for Gaynor.

"Have you missed us then?"

"What do you think?"

"So, what did you get up to?"
It was then that he burst out laughing.

"Dad, has something happened?"

"You could say that."

"Well, are you going to tell us or not?"

"Of course I am. Please, just give me a minute."
Aware of his penchant for practical jokes and surprises, they waited. At last, he managed to say,

"Gaynor, do you remember when Ellie was born and you said that you felt something brush past you as you were giving her a bath?"

"Yes, it was very benign and caring. Why?"

"Well, this is going to sound crazy, but it was my mum."
His wife and daughter looked at one another quizzically. Eventually, it was Gaynor who broke the ice.

"I thought that you didn't believe in the supernatural? And, anyway, how do you know that it was her?"

"Well, first of all, the supernatural doesn't cease to exist just because I don't believe in it and second, because I saw her. She was here in the flat and we spoke to one another. In fact, we've talked every day for the past few days."

Still more quizzical looks.

"Dad, this isn't one of your jokes, is it?"

He shook his head, "No, it's not." He smiled, "It really happened."

Perhaps they believed him but, more likely, they decided to humour him.

Gaynor looked at him intently. "How, Mike and why now after all these years?"

He tried hard not to look serious and just to be so.

"You believe me then?"

"Well, you're obviously not joking so, yes, I do although I don't understand. It's funny but, in some ways I'm not surprised. Is she coming back?"

He broke out into a broad grin. "Just as soon as I call her. She wants to meet you if that's OK?"

They both looked at him in utter amazement, "What's she like?"

"She's lovely and we haven't stopped talking. It's as if she'd never died in the first place. Like a dream come true. Mary Rose"

"But how and why now."

"She's one of the unresolveds, a ghost who needs to be resolved so that she can rest in peace. Die properly, in fact. I just have to call her for her to materialise. It's easy really although tiring to maintain and, after a while, we can't hold it together any longer and she goes back to the cemetery with the others."

"But why now?"

"It's to do with the anniversary. It's 70 years, you know. I had this vivid dream and an insistent voice in my head asking me to call. Eventually it got so strong that I did just that and there she was."

"For how long?"

"For a few hours each time."

"No, I meant how long have you got together?"

"Until she's resolved at which point there won't be sufficient to keep her here. She thinks about just over a week, the time between her death and the funeral. That's when the need is stronger."

"That's not very long. Can't you keep it going for longer?"

"Well we can keep it up but, as I said, it's the strength of our combined emotion keeps us together and that determines when she's resolved. From what they know of the other ghosts, it's been about a week or so. Perhaps we'll be different although we need to be ready for the worst case scenario."

"You've had plenty of practice at that over the years, Mike. In fact it's your modus operandum to be ready for the worst."
He smiled, "Well in that case, it should stand me in good stead. I'm rather relying on the fact that we're both ready for it at the same time. Still we'll see when it happens."
"So, what does she look like?"

"She looks just like her photo and she really wants to meet you both."

"This really isn't one of your practical jokes, is it?"

"No, I'm deadly serious although, perhaps, deadly isn't the best way to describe it."
They both looked at one another again still hardly able to believe that they were having this conversation with one of life's ultimate rationalists.
"Well, if you've already had a number of visits, we may not have much longer so let's get on with it."
Even in the strangest of circumstances, his wife's practical side asserted itself. As he was about to call her, he had

a sudden thought that three of the most important people in his life, all women, were about to be in the same room together. It surely couldn't get much better than this.

"OK, Mum, we're ready."

And there she was. Shy, smiling and trying hard not to cry.

"Mum, this is Gaynor and this is Ellie, your youngest granddaughter." He hugged her, both with the sheer joy of the occasion and to let them know that, for him, it was the most natural thing to do. Even with a ghost.

A little hesitantly, they embraced before sitting down unsure of what to do next. Fortunately she decided to break the ice.

"Hello, Ellie, it seems that we share the same name."

"Yes, I was named after you, almost. My middle name is Louise whereas I think that you're Louisa."

"Yes but everyone called me Lou when I was alive although Gran would be nice right now. If that's alright?"

He found himself smiling as were the others. Mutual pleasure. She did, however, look extremely young for the grandmother of a 23 year old alongside a son and a daughter in law who were a generation older than her. On a similar wavelength as him she said, "I may look 34 but actually I'm really over 100."

"Mum, one of dad's sisters, Eileen, lived to be nearly 105 so, in other circumstances, you might well have still been alive. Just." Funny how he used the word "dad" and not "my father" when Gaynor and Ellie were around.

"And from what I've seen of what you have in your home, what wonders I might have witnessed."

He nodded in acknowledgement of the enormous social and technological changes that he'd been lucky enough to have been part of. Sad that she'd missed them.

"Gaynor, Mike has told me quite a lot about how you two met and, Ellie, about your childhood but not a lot since then. Are you still teaching? It must be very satisfying. And you, Ellie, what are you doing with yourself?"

107

It seems that she wasn't going to take the chance that the conversation wouldn't take off, at which he was delighted. He needn't have worried. There may have been a big difference between working class women from 70 years ago and their children and grandchildren today, but there was still their shared female experience. That, unspoken bond, if nothing else, stood them in good stead. Sitting there, watching them, brought back childhood memories of family parties and the solidarity of "the sisters" in his father's family, Ada, Sylvie, Eileen, Ellen, Thora, Kath and Doreen. It also reminded him of what his father had cut himself off from for the whole of his adult life. And, again, he asked himself "Why?" in somewhat stronger terms that that simple word might signify. WTF might have been more apposite.

Along the way, his mother found out about Gaynor's family, Ellie's childhood, her school days and university and, a particular delight, her choice of writing as a career. So there wouldn't be one but two authors in the family. With ten siblings of her own and another ten in her husband's family, along with the length of time since she's last spoken to any of them, she would be forgiven for finding it difficult to keep track of these new generations. "So, remind me again, who is Chris? And Amy?" To find out that there was another Michael, her great grandson, now 16, was icing on the cake.

What was particularly a joy for him, was seeing the interaction between three generations, his mother, his wife and his youngest daughter. Mirrored, he felt, in her own at the whole situation. All to a background of smiles, laughter and tears. Whoever talked about the peace of the grave, never took account of the sounds of the living simply taking pleasure in each others' company. So, perhaps best not to think about the future now and just enjoy what they had.

After what must have been nearly an hour, he went into the kitchen to make tea and coffee and, looking over into the tableau in the living room, took a quick shot on his mobile. Would he have the first, guaranteed genuine, photo of a ghost? Well, nearly. There was something although, to be honest, it could have been any one of those much loved by spiritualists with its lack of clarity. Just as well, really. This wasn't for public consumption.

As he brought the cups in he noticed that he was feeling, not so much tired but more, lacking in energy. He looked over to his mother to see that she was signaling him with her eyes. She was feeling it too. Her visit was coming to an end. Somehow, it had come upon them barely noticed. At which point he had the thought that, maybe, the sheer joy of them all being together had disguised the extra effort required to enable that to happen. Yet, despite the "bad" news, he was delighted that they had quickly built up the rapport with his mother that they would both have hoped for. Then he looked up again to realise that what concerned his mother wasn't leaving but disappointing Gaynor and Ellie. This feeling of empathy was, he knew, a flashback to times past when a small child recognised his mother's tiredness and tried to alleviate it.

"Gaynor, Ellie, Mum's a bit tired so, we may have to curtail the meeting for today. I'm sorry."
She looked over at the pair of them before reaching out to take their hands in hers. From the looks on their faces, they too weren't ready for this. They couldn't help, however, but notice the signs.

"I'm sorry but I have to go. Being all together has taken more out of Michael and me than I'd thought. Still, I'll see you tomorrow. Take care. Bye, Ellie. Bye Gaynor. Bye, my child. Love you." Then she was gone and the room felt empty as they returned to the real world that, right now, felt as if it was an intrusion.

As they all sat there with their own thoughts, his feelings were that this was as good as it got. Not for him the Long Lost Families that didn't get on very well together afterwards. He knew that he hadn't really expected anything to go wrong as he knew that both his wife and his daughter would always make every effort. What he'd been worried about was something that he had no real experience of. Had they not got on well, were would his loyalties have lain? He needn't have worried.

"Now how about some lunch? Soup in about twenty minutes?"

The kitchen had always been therapeutic for him and it was now. Wash up a couple of cups, prepare the veg, stick them in the pan, season and the soup was ready. While he was doing that, he could hear Ellie and Gaynor talking; a mixture of disbelieve and laughter from two people on the same wavelength. Soon, now that the other wordly personage had gone, to be joined by Midnight.

As they sat down to eat, the conversation continued. He'd learnt over the years that it was unwise to make adverse comments about other peoples' loved ones, especially their parents, so he'd expected his wife's usual courtesy. What he got, however, was what he'd hoped for, genuine affection from both of them. It seemed that things could only get better after all.

When they went to bed that night, their conversation was in a similar vein. So, his mother was loved by others.
She was a good person and not (Michael, are you listening?) one who abandoned him!

Learning to be Normal

The following day, after Gaynor and Ellie had left for work, he felt a familiar, insistent female voice in his head.

Michael, call me, please. As soon as you can.

Just a minute, Mum.

Michael, could you please call me?

OK, Mum. You'd best come in.

"My, you're impatient this morning. I thought you said that you needed time to recover."

"Come on, what did you expect. After all, it's not often that a ghost gets to meet her daughter in law and granddaughter. And, yes, I do know that this may be a slightly shorter visit but I need to know?"

"I get that but, tell me, what did the others say?"

"Just what you'd expect. What were they like? Did you get on well with them? Do they love him? Are they happy together?" Fortunately, I was able to reassure them on all points. So, as you might say "brownie points all round.""

111

"Where did you pick that up?"

"One of my friends. I'd never heard it before, so I asked her what it meant. It seems right."

He smiled, "Yeah, it is. I use it a lot. So, you OK?"

She smiled back, "You could say that. You know life may not have always dealt me the best of hands but the past few days have more than made up for it. Unfortunately it's also made me sad."

"Yes, I know. What might have been? Like I said, it was the theme tune to my life for most of it. It still is despite what I now have. I guess that knowing what I might have done has always driven me."

"Well, what did they make of me?"

"What do you think? They loved you."

"You're not just saying that, are you?"

"Mum, you talked together for over an hour. Until, in fact, we were drained."

"Really. Wow, so we've managed to hold it together for three real people. Maybe I shouldn't have worried so much after all."

"That does tend to be somewhat of a family trait and, given the circumstances, quite understandable."

"So, what's for today, my son?"

"Do you know I'm not sure. You see, if we were meeting in real life much of the time we wouldn't be talking. We'd be just sitting together, going out for a walk, reading, playing games, watching television or whatever. With us, it's packing a whole lifetime into a few days. It's like we have no time to breathe. Just to enjoy each other's company."

"What do you suggest?"

"I'm not sure. It's difficult creating a normal situation from an unusual one. I remember when I got divorced and there were two others in the office in the same boat. They were envious of the fact that I'd got custody of Tracey and Matt whereas they only got to see their kids at weekends. They both said that what was difficult was the feeling that everything had to be perfect every minute that they were together. What they dreaded was having any sort of discord and then having to wait until the following week to make up for it. It didn't make for an easy time."

"How about watching television. Now that would be fun. Something to tell the others."

"I tell you what. Let me read a little more and then I'll check out what's on and you can pick something."

"I'd like that, Michael."

"So where were we?"

"You'd just got divorced and moved to Harrogate to start a new life."

"Mum, I hope that my memory's as good as yours when I'm your age."

"Michael" she smiled, "That's outrageous." At which point they both burst out laughing.

"Before we start, do you mind if I make myself some toast and a cup of tea as I've not had anything to eat yet."

"Off you go and let me know when you're ready."

"OK. Won't be a couple of minutes."
When he looked back, she was looking at the bookshelves.
"I meant to say this earlier but you've got lots of books. We never had any in our house. Couldn't afford them even when they started selling them in paperback."

"When was that?"

"A few years before the war, I think. Your father used to get his poetry from the library."

"There aren't many libraries any more, although there are lots of bookshops. That's where we get ours from."

"Why do you have so many?"

"I can't throw books away. Even lending them to friends is difficult. They're part of my history and I need to keep them. The same with records and, what we call, CD's."

"Those things?" she said pointing.

"Yep, those. My music and my books, they're important to me. They represent what I've been and who I am. The ones I've written, especially, mean that I'll leave a record behind for my family, including those who've not even been born yet. I like that.

"I don't seem to have left anything."

"You did, Mum, you left me and I love you for that. In fact, that's probably the reason why I'm the way I am. So thank you for that because I now like what I am and what I've done. It's also why I keep going. That's not a bad legacy to leave, is it?"
She smiled somewhat ruefully. "Maybe I'd like to have done something other than what I did. I never thought about that before."

"Mum, I'm not saying this just because you're here but every generation stands on the shoulders of the previous one. Your generation had the broadest of shoulders ever. They went through a war, for heaven's sake. They've even been called "the finest generation". Isn't that something to be proud of?"

"It does when you say it like that although, at the time, we just wanted to get to the next day."

"You getting through to the next day ensured that there would be a next day for us. So, yes, you have more to be proud of than most."
She looked him directly in the eyes. "You certainly have your father's way with words, Michael, but it's still nice to hear you say it."
This, making her happy, did feel good.
"The book? OK, but please let me know if it becomes a bit much, won't you? So, we'd just moved to Harrogate so that I could become a fulltime student. What I now refer to as the start of the rest of my life."
Best not to mention the sex and drugs.
"I'm all ears."
The next hour passed with her still managing to appear to be listening intently, something he commented on.
"Michael, please I am enjoying it. It may not be easy for a mother to hear how difficult it had been for her child but I like hearing about what you did. Anyways, it's getting better now."

"Sorry, Mum, it does get bad again but, ultimately, I'm happy and, with you here, even happier."

"So, have we got time for anything else?"

"A little bit of television might be nice. What is there?"

"Mum, what isn't there? There are hundreds of channels all day. Documentaries, news, sport, film, dramas, comedy, quizzes. You name it and we have it. Unfortunately, most of it's rubbish"

"How do you choose?"
He laughed. "By avoiding the rubbish and trying to find something interesting. So, what will I look for?"
"Well, I always liked dancing."

115

"No, no, this can't be. Not "Strictly."

So, after a scroll down and look at other programmes until, "Strictly" it was, on catch up. And he remained quiet while his mother sat enthralled. Although, it has to be said, she was somewhat taken aback by the inadequate nature of the women's clothing. Not, she noted, matched by that of the men. Yes, she had insisted, skirts had risen to just below the ankle in her day but she certainly hadn't expected this.

She would have watched for hours except that the pull from the other side got stronger and their emotional effort weakened. Eventually, after a bit of "Fools and Horses", they had to acknowledge that, it was time to call is a day.

"Can you tell Gaynor and Ellie that I was asking after them and that it would be nice to see them again soon."

"Of course. Love you, Mum."

"Love you, Michael."

As she faded from view, he had the usual feeling of sadness and, 'if only' while being grateful for this opportunity. If only, if only. Would that feeling ever leave him entirely? Before another thought came into his head. The strength of their involvement showed no signs of abating so, maybe they could extend their time together. Just a thought.

When they got home that evening, Gaynor and Ellie were, as might be imagined, keen to know when they could see his mother again. It was then that he had to explain how she was so impatient to know how they felt about her that she had insisted that he call her earlier in the day.

"So she's already been?"

"It was only meant to be a fleeting visit, but……."
They both laughed.

"It's OK, Dad, this is for you. You've waited your whole life but, obviously, we'd like to see her again. And we might not get many more opportunities."

"Tomorrow then?"

"Tomorrow. Anyway, what did you talk about?"

"Well we talked about trying to make the visits more normal. You know, when we go to stay with Tracey we don't sit down talking about the past all the time. Sometimes we read, watch TV or go out for a walk."

"From what she's told us, the last of these is out of the question so how did you make the rest of it normal?"

"We watched television."

"Fairly normal then. What did you watch?"

"Well, once she'd got over the shock of seeing just how much choice there was, I asked her what she liked and she told me that she'd always loved dancing."

"Dad, you didn't watch 'Strictly?'"

"Of course. My mother wanted to so we did. Mind you she was a bit dumbfounded by the fact that the women hardly wore any clothing and that what they did wear was rather revealing. She was, obviously, aware of how much things had changed in her own lifetime but this was beyond anything that she could have imagined."

"Was she shocked then?"

"I think so although she tried not to show it."

"Then we watched an early episode of 'Fools and Horses', which she quite enjoyed, and just about got to the end before we couldn't hold it together anymore."

"So next time will also be more normal then."

"Yep."

"Then why don't you arrange it so that we can join you when we get home."

"That sounds like a good idea. Can you both be home tomorrow night at six then?"

"Yes, no problem."

"OK, I'll call her at about 5 and hope that we can sustain things as long as we normally do. Can you both text me when you're on your way?"

"OK."

"OK."

"Now, what do you want for supper?"

Discovering
Modern Living

The following morning, after the usual routine, he sat down to write. Unfortunately, he couldn't get thoughts of just how long they would have together out of his head. Eventually he could wait no longer.

Mum, can I speak to you for a moment, please?
No sooner said than done and there she was.

"Michael, what's up? Is something wrong?"

"Not so much wrong, Mum, as something that I need to get clearer before this evening when Gaynor and Ellie would like to meet you again."

"That will be nice". She smiled in a way that he'd come to recognise. "Now what is it that you wanted to talk about?"

"Mum, it's that thing about just how long we've got together. I know I'm being a pain but not knowing causes me real problems. When we first talked about it you said that you thought that it might be about a week or so. Well, we're over half way there and the feeling between us seems as strong as ever."

"Yes, it does. It's something that the others are quite surprised about. They don't think, though, that that'll make a great deal of difference in the end. Yes, the reason that we can do this is so that I can be resolved and the emotion between us is very strong but so is the pull from the emotions surrounding the anniversary of the funeral."

"Yes I get that but how can an event that took place all those years ago and was attended by people who're now dead themselves, have that power?"

"I wish I knew, my child. All that we can come up with is that, my spiritual death is controlled by the same conditions that my physical one was. My body couldn't hold out any longer and neither will me spirit be able to. I'm sorry."

"So am I, Mum, so am I."
She reached out to hold him and that gave him great comfort. He felt like a small child again. The one that existed before that Mike came on the scene. As she continued to hold him, he felt the adult taking over. An adult with that resilience and determination to keep going, no matter what. Her arms fell away as if she, too, could feel something happening and she looked at him to see that he was smiling.
"It'll be OK, Mum. At least we'll have had this. I can settle for that. She smiled back. "You always were a determined little bugger."

"I wonder where I got that from?"
He could hardly have said anything better to make her feel that her time on Earth had been more than just a fight against a lifetime of poverty and sickness. Trying not to look too delighted, she said, "I did talk to the others and they say that they haven't noticed anything yet."
"What would they be looking for?"

"Well, for a start, problems in getting through to me when they want to talk followed by me having difficulty in remembering what's being said and having less energy."

120

"Ghosts have Dementia? I don't believe this!"

"Michael, I'm a simple girl from Mud Island, what's Dementia?"

"It's alright, Mum, it was just a joke, albeit one in rather bad taste. It's a serious 21st century condition, one of whose symptoms is memory loss."

"So, you feel better about it now?"

"A bit. My real worry though was that it would happen without warning and that seems not to be likely. So, yeah, I can manage with that. Thanks."

"You don't need to thank me for doing what any parent should do for their children. Will you call me later."

"Of course. Love you."

"Love you too."
As she disappeared, he thought that, maybe, this 'being normal' could work. Ah, well, back to the grindstone, although that phrase was one that he had long since ceased to use to describe his work. It was to be another six hours before he called her when he hoped that she would still be strong and that the normality would continue. Finally, at 5 o'clock precisely, he called her.
Mum, it's me. OK to meet?
"I'm here, Michael and still not senile."
Like him, he suspected that, although the quick wit was natural, it had been honed by adversity. No wonder they got on well together.

"Gaynor and Ellie will be home by six, so we'll all have some time together. Is that OK?"

"Of course."
Be natural, Mike. You don't have to act, this is your mum.

The person who changed your nappy. Anyway, you've all been together already so don't make it more than it is. This is not a situation where you're the odd one out or there's someone in your house that you feel uncomfortable with. Just relax.

"How're you feeling, Mum?"

"I'm fine and the others send their love."

"That's nice. Tell them ditto."
Relax. You don't have to have a plan to talk to her.
"Michael, is something wrong? You seem a bit distant."
What was wrong? They'd talked all week and done the normal things that people do together normally. She'd met his family and now they just had to continue that. Why was this difficult now?
It was then that he had an uncomfortable feeling about being in their house in Edale Road. There were a lot of strangers but not his mum. There weren't any other children and the adults were talking quietly, not with their usual loud voices. It didn't feel good. He hadn't had therapy for all those years not to realise the cause of his discomfort. He'd also had enough about himself to know that today wasn't a repeat of that particular occasion. This was different. It was today, it was his house and it was his family. It was normal. At least as normal as meeting a ghost could be. At that, he smiled.

"It's alright, Mum, I was miles away. I'm fine, why wouldn't I be?
I hope.

"Mum, I'm going to get the supper ready soon so do you want me to put something on the television for you to watch while I'm doing that. We'll still be able to talk."

"Sounds fine to me. What is there?"

"I thought that you might like 'Call the Midwife'. It's not exactly my cup of tea but it's the story of midwives in Poplar in the 1950's, based on the memoirs of one of them."

"That sounds nice. Can you put it on for me, please?"

"No problem."

Well that was the next hour sorted and they could still chat over the worktop.

As the opening title came up, she asked, "Do you enjoy cooking? None of the men in our family did that, you know."

"I suspect that none of them worked from home either and, yes, I do remember what it was like. When I was a child, you never saw a man pushing a pram and, if you saw anyone with a beard, the likelihood was that they were in the Navy. Women were housewives and, as for black people, well they lived in Brixton. Today's world is very different. We've still a very long way to go but we do have a more equal society and that feels good. Mind you, nobody mentioned anything about people being gay."

"Gay, what does that mean?"

"Sorry, Mum, it's a term used to describe someone who's homosexual."
She smiled. "You mean like Bob?"
"I thought so. Was he gay?"

"We always thought so but we never asked and he never said."

"I understand that he wanted to adopt me but my father wasn't keen on the idea."

"He loved you, Michael, and looked after you."

"Yes, I know. I met him once years later when he was very ill and living in Gifford Street. I think his daughter was with him. He died soon after."
She looked crestfallen but quickly shook it off. "Silly of me, they're all dead now anyway so that should hardly be news. Still, it is sad. I just needed more time with all of you."

"I can't make it all better for you, Mum, but, in the

meantime, we can enjoy what we have."

"We can indeed. So, can I get back to, what was it, 'The Midwife'?"

"'Call the Midwife', Mum. It's one of Gaynor's favourites."
Five minutes later and he looked over to see her, engrossed.
"You enjoying that?"

"Shush, Michael, I'm watching."
He smiled and carried on chopping the onions. This was indeed normal and, so far, it was proving to be surprisingly easy. Half an hour later, with the Shepherd's Pie in the oven and the washing up done, he walked back into the sitting room.
"Mind if I join you?"

"Michael, you don't have to ask for permission, it's your house."

"Eey, Moother, ah were brought oop proper." Now the normality was real. He was doing those impressions and funny accents that Gaynor would have been so familiar with.

"I know, I brought you up. As long as I was able to."
He sat down next to her on the sofa. "Now, Mum, I thought that we'd already dealt with that."
Now all he had to do was not make too many comments on the programme itself and to try to look as though he was interested. As he'd expected, although the prominence of the realistic portrayal of childbirth took her by surprise, she did find television fascinating. As he himself had done when he first watched it. In his case, for the Coronation of 1953 in that flat above a butcher's shop in Old Kent Road. He was taken out of his reverie by the sound of the doorbell.
"That'll be Ellie. Gaynor probably has her keys."

"That'll be nice."

At which time, the next shock arrived for her. Her grand-daughter wearing a pair of headphones in the form of cat's ears. How much more explaining would they have to do? Needless to say, she was fascinated and the questions (and a demonstration) followed. Both grandmother and grand-daughter were in their element. Then he heard the key in the lock and Gaynor arrived home from work.

"What've you two been doing?"

"Well I've been cooking the supper while mum (it was lovely to be able to say that in day to day conversation) has been watching 'Call the Midwife'.
Both Gaynor and Ellie smiled. "What did you think, Lou?"

"I liked it. It was very true to life and I felt as if I was alive again. And to have all this in your sitting room when-ever you want. It's amazing. I thought the cinema was spe-cial but this much more so. And you have your own, Ellie, and you all have computers." She used this word as the very unfamiliar one that it was too her.

"Do you want to have a go, Granny? I could show you?"

"Really? Now that would be something to tell the others although I'm not sure how I would even begin to explain it. What do I do?"

"Dad, can we use the desktop as there's room there for both of us to sit?"

"No problem. I'll just log in."
His mother looked a little quizzical at this but sat down anyway.
"OK, Granny, let's start by typing a letter."

At which point, he and Gaynor went to sit down on the sofa with a glass of wine each and the television on. Quietly delighting in watching a granddaughter teach her grand-mother about 21st century life. This really was normal, pro-vided that you could ignore the fact that the grandmother had been dead for 70 years! Another hour was to pass before he felt the tiredness pulling at him and noticed that his mother was becoming less animated.

"Mum."

"It's OK, Michael, I know. And, just to set your mind at rest, it's seems to me just like a normal tired end to a visit." She reached over to hug Ellie with absolute delight in her eyes. Something that was, of course, reciprocated.

"Thank you, Ellie. See you tomorrow and you, Gaynor. And, of course, you, my child." She hugged Gaynor and him and slipped away leaving them all a little lost for words.

"Supper, anyone?"

Later, when they'd eaten, they had time to think about what had happened.

"You really did think that I was pulling one enormous practical joke didn't you?"

"Well, what did you expect with your track record and what you were asking us to believe?"

"I suppose so."

"But then, when she really appeared. Well it was amazing but a bit scary. Wasn't it for you? You've always said that you don't believe in ghosts while, at the same time, being very scared of them."

"Yes I never worked that out myself although I'm pretty sure that it had something to do with seeing her face as I looked into the coffin."

"How could anyone have thought that that was a good idea?"

"Different times, love. Nowadays the whole thing takes place away from the home whereas, in those days, people died and were then made ready, laid out, in the front room.

Flowers were brought in to mask the smell. If nothing else, it was cheaper and they had no money at the best of times. One of my cousins told me that her parents didn't even have shoes as children and largely lived on what their father brought home from the slaughterhouse."

"It sounds like something out of Monty Python. You know, that sketch about "We were so poor, we lived in a shoebox.""

"And I used to think that it was my dad's family who were poor. Now I realise they must have had some assets as they came from a long line of coopers in Ireland to set up a business over here. It would explain what I've heard about how some in the families regarded one another."

"Anyway, enough of the family history, where do we go from here?"

"Surely that will depend on when your mum feels resolved and we don't know when that will be, do we?

"Well, we can only go on what she's been told. That it might be about a week and a half. The time between the death and the funeral. And we've already had a week. So, and I'm trying to be as objective as possible, I'm not thinking beyond next weekend. If we get longer that's a bonus."

She had lived with him for long enough to know both the rationalisation then the acceptance of reality. In that order. She was also very worried about just what effect his mother leaving for good would have. Yes, as he always did, he'd manage but what might it drag up from the past? He looked at her and smiled. "Don't worry, I'll be OK. After all, I have you." What she did notice, however, when they went to bed that night is that he held her a little tighter than normal. And she wasn't surprised.

An Early Morning Visit

The following morning he sat in front of the desktop alternating between trying to write and playing Solitaire.

Michael, can you call me?

"OK, Mum. Please come in."

As soon as she appeared, he noticed that she looked a little awkward. "Is everything alright?"

"Yes, of course it is except…."

"Except what, Mum? What's wrong?"

She looked at the floor. "Nothing's wrong. I just wondered if you were busy."

"Not for you. I'm trying to write but I can do that anytime. I like peace and quiet but I write when Gaynor and Ellie are home and even when they have the television on."

She smiled at that.

He smiled back in response. "You want to watch 'Strictly' again?"

"No. But 'Call the Midwife' would be nice, if that's OK."

"Won't that make it more difficult for you to visit tonight when Gaynor and Ellie are here?"

"I'm not sure although I noticed that just watching your television last night took less out of me than when we do a lot of talking. So, I hope not and, if it does, I won't do it again. Although that would be a shame for the others."

"You told them?"

"Obviously, the passing on of what we learn is important in keeping our hopes up. It helps us to get on together. By the way, are there many episodes of this?"

"Many more than we have time for I should think."

"That's a shame. I was rather hoping that I could see all of them by the time I'm resolved."

"Unless we have weeks in front of us, that's unlikely. The last series Gaynor watched was number eight, I think, and each series went on for about eight weeks."

"That many. Oh well."

"Mum, it doesn't matter too much as the episodes are each a story of their own so just watch as many as you can."

"How do I turn it on?"

"Please, sit down. I'll do it."
So, with his mother watching television and him sat nearby at the desktop, they could have been any mother visiting her son while looking like a young woman visiting an older relative. Albeit a young woman that, anyone watching would have noticed, the older man always deferred to. An hour later and, reluctantly, she agreed that her visit should be curtailed so that they could meet again this evening.
"It'll be OK. I'm sure Gaynor and Ellie will be up for

watching another episode even if they've seen it before."

"If you're sure, that would be nice. Could you ask them for me?"

"Of course. See you this evening?"

"Love you, Michael."

"Love you, Mum."

And, with that, she was gone and he had to try to get back to normal. Wherever that was, now and in the future. Perhaps a cup of coffee and some day to day tasks would help. Newspaper, crossword and coffee, followed by trying to concentrate on his writing. Finally, at about five, he decided to get the supper ready. All normal. Eventually, a little tired he decided to catnap for five minute only to be woken by the doorbell. Six o'clock and Ellie obviously hadn't taken her keys that morning.

"What time will Granny be visiting?"

"She already did this morning to catch up on "Call the Midwife."

The picture of one delighted daughter would stay with him for a long while.

"No!"

"Yes. Anyway I'll call her at about seven. How was your day?"

"The new job is good and I'm enjoying it. Better than working in a shop, that's for sure."

"We'll have supper at about eightish. Shepherd's Pie OK?"

"Yeah, please."

And, with that, she was off into her room. Half an hour later and a key in the lock heralded Gaynor's return. So he put the kettle on.

"You OK, love?"

"Just the usual. You?"

"Well, I had an interesting conversation with my mother this morning."

"I thought that she'd visit this evening?"
Wasn't it strange how all of them were talking about a ghost visiting as if it was the most normal thing in the world. Or in her world either?

"She will but this was because she had something special that she needed to ask me."

"Well you don't look as though it was bad news."
He laughed, "No, she just asked if she could watch another episode of 'Call the Midwife'. She and all the others wanted to know what happened."

"So?"

"I put on the TV and worked while she watched. I thought that was wonderfully normal. Some sign of resolution. So, I feel pleased, if a little apprehensive."

"I can imagine."

"So, don't be upset or surprised if…."

"I won't. Do you want supper or shall I call her now?"

"Supper would be nice as I'm peckish and I could do with a sit down."

"OK. Ellie, supper's ready.
Half an hour later, with a glass of wine in hand, he called.
"Mum, are you there?"
Seconds later and she was.

"Now where were we?"

"Well, you were watching 'Call the Midwife'.
She smiled along with a long, drawn out "Yes." Then, "But not this evening. If Gaynor and Ellie don't mind, could you read more to me and could I hear something that Ellie has written?"
He looked around to see his daughter smiling. "Ellie?"
"I'd love to. Let me find something."
He followed as she walked into her bedroom. "Have you got something appropriate."

"Of course. It'll just take me a minute to find it. Don't worry."
He walked back into the living room moving to one side to avoid his mother who was walking in the other direction.
Make yourself at home, Mum.
Through the half open door, he could hear her asking her granddaughter about her writing and Ellie explaining to her what a laptop was and how to use the mouse, before finding a suitable story.
"Here we are. This should be OK."

"How many have you got?"

"Loads. I just type them on here and then save them. Like I showed you yesterday. Anyway, this ones called 'Read On' and it's a story about how there's a book describing how each person's life is and what happens when they get the chance to read about what will happen to them."

"I'm not sure that I'd have liked that."

"Me neither but I just thought that it would make a good story. It's not finished but you can read what I've written so far. When you get as far as you can, scroll down like I said, and continue reading."
Apart from the first time, when she had to ask how to scroll down, they hardly heard a word for half an hour. One person, it would seem, enjoying what she was reading and the

other delighting in her interest. Eventually, he heard his mother say, "Did you imagine all this?"

"Yes, like Dad, I have an idea and I just write what comes into my head. Unlike Dad, I did have some training at university."

"I remember even as a small child, he had a lively imagination but, then, don't all children have that?"

"I suppose so and most can make up stories. Did he do that?"

"Yes, all the time. Mind you, his father had a way with words…."

"The gift of the gab, I think it's called. I remember when we went to Ireland once and Dad put his head through a hole on the wall to kiss the Blarney Stone. Mum said he didn't really need to do that."

"Like father, like son."
Outside, his wife noticed him listening to the conversation.
"You OK?"

"Yeah, of course. Isn't that lovely?" he said, nodding towards the door.
A short while later, his mother emerged with a rueful smile on her face. "This generation are aware of a great deal more than I ever was."

"More than mine too. Do you feel up to more reading?"

"Before I do, can you show me more of what you can watch on the television. I'd like to tell the others."
So what followed was scrolling up and down, 'Catch Up' and 'On Demand' before she settled on 'Long Lost Families'.

"Do you think I could watch that tomorrow?"

"Of course. Morning or evening?"

"I'll let you know but, before I go, do you think that Gaynor and me might get some time together?"

"Why not?" he said while thinking "Why?"

"I'll just get a book and adjourn to the spare room so you can have some privacy."

"Are you sure?"

"Yes, Mum, it's fine."
Twenty minutes later and they both came out smiling. "Find out what you wanted to know?" At which point he found out, if he didn't already know, that his characteristic of telling people everything, wasn't something that his wife and mother shared with him.

"Now, before I go, just a little bit more from your book? Something about how your life changed, maybe?"

"OK, let jump a little to when I started working for my first charity."

"That sounds nice."
Fortunately they were able to finish the chapter before the bond between them started to weaken.

"Michael, I think I need to go."

"OK. See you tomorrow. Morning or afternoon?"

"Gaynor, Ellie, I'm off now. See you tomorrow?"

"See you, Lou."
Ellie's bedroom door opened as she came out to give her grandmother a hug; much to his mum's delight.

"See you tomorrow, Granny."
And she was gone.
He followed his daughter back into her room to give her a hug before he and Gaynor decided to do nothing more than watch the television.
Later, when they were in bed, he asked, "What did you two talk about?"

"Nothing that you shouldn't know. She just wanted to know if you were happy and I told her that I thought that you were."

"Thank you, my love, I am.

"You know if you want to go back to seeing her on your own again, that will be fine."

"Yes, I know. Would that be OK with Ellie?"

"Yes, it would. We have talked and the bottom line is that this is for you. Although you do still need to sort out what to tell Tracey and Matt."

"I know. Sleep well, my love."

"You too."
Just before he fell asleep, he reflected that his new normality involved his daughter reading to her grandmother, his wife and his mother having a tete a tete and all of them watching television together. It could have been any extended family, except that it wasn't. It was, in fact, a rather unusual one. His dreams that night were of the ghosts of others he knew who'd died, some of whom seemed to think that he could help them too. You could have called it a restless night.

Another Early Morning Visit

The following morning, he resolved that he would tell his eldest children what was happening. After all, how would he face them afterwards when she would no longer be around? The problem was how to get them all together; a gathering of his whole family all under one roof. Then the penny dropped big time. The technology that she's taken such a shine to. First, though, he'd need to talk to Matt or Chris to see if they thought that it might be possible; and to his mum to see how she felt about the idea. The latter of these, he thought, should be a formality. The former he wasn't sure about. And it wasn't just about the technology. After all, in the past few days he, a rationalist if nothing else, had actually been talking to a ghost. And, yes, he'd seen photographic images that purported to be of ghosts but they'd never looked very convincing. So, after some thought, he rang his grandson.

Now, Chris had studied physics at university, even going on to do his MSc, so logic and rationale were his bread and butter. He reasoned that a Skype call was usually merely a means of transmission whereas a photograph was actually a record; something that might make a difference. If the call wasn't recorded, his mum's image was, in fact, a series of still photographs, one after the other. It wouldn't matter if each one faded. QED as his old Maths teacher would have said. Anyway, it was worth a try. So, get his newspaper, then breakfast and coffee and time to think. Then he would call her. As, half an hour later, he did.

"Mum, I need to speak to you. Can you come over, please?"

"Michael, why have you called? Is something wrong?"

"No, Mum, not wrong, it's just that I have a problem and an idea of how we might solve it. I just need to talk to you first to see if you think that it's possible."

"What's possible?"

"Well, you know that Tracey and Matt and your great grandchildren live too far away for us all to be able to meet?"

"Yes?"
And you said that the emotion of others can help sustain you here. In this realm, I think you called it?"
She looked at him quizzically. "Yes?"
"And that, when I took a photo of you all on my mobile phone, although it captured your image too when we replayed it, both your voice and the image were gone."

"You didn't tell me you'd done that? Or that your phone could take photographs. How is that possible."

"Mum, it can take moving photo's. Films. What we call video."

"Yes?"

"And, finally, I can make a video phone call to a whole group of people. Now, although the image won't be

137

permanent, it will be there momentarily . Long enough for them to see you."

"Michael, I'm sorry but I'm actually someone from a different age and, at times like this, I find it difficult to understand what you're talking about."

"Mum, anybody would. Perhaps a demonstration would help. Let me ring Ellie at work."
She still looked confused.
Fortunately his youngest daughter had already had a similar thought but was waiting for a good time to broach the subject. She was also aware that her father was also more receptive when he'd thought things through himself. Or thought that he had!
"Ellie, can we show mum what a Skype call is like and think hard about her while you're making it.?"

"We can if you can remember how to do it."

"Remind me." So she did and a few minutes later, there she was, smiling, on the desktop.
His mother had to sit down. How on earth was this possible? Well, she knew that she was on earth, so maybe it could be. And she was seeing it, so it was.
"Say something, Mum."

"Ellie, is that you? Where are you?"

"I'm at work and, yes, it's me." She smiled broadly.

"How are you able to do that?"

"Granny, you've watched television? Well this is similar. It's not magic."

"Ellie!"

"Sorry, Granny, but my generation does this all the time. We use Skype, Zoom, Wire, Facetime and any number of other apps, which will have been added to even as we speak. Basically, it's a phone call with pictures."

"And you're thinking that I might be able to talk to my other grandchildren like this?"

"Well, we've managed it now so, why not? Anyway, I have to go. I've got things to do before the end of the day. See you later."
And with that, the screen went blank.
"Michael."

"Yes, Mum."

"Do you mind if I watch some television before I go back?"

"Of course not, 'Open All Hours' OK?"
Ten minutes later and he could hear her laughing at something that he liked; another instance of something shared. Another episode of "Midwife" during which he broached the matter of conserving her energy for this evening.
"Do you mind if I just watch the end of this first?"
He smiled. It was getting more normal as the time passed, until, that is, he thought of just the time that was passing. Ten minutes later, engrossed in something he was writing, he heard her say. "See you this evening, my child." He looked up as she kissed him before she slipped away. "Love you, Mum." And then she was gone. Now to get on with what he'd started. Not too difficult as he'd just thought of a good ending for something that he was writing and needed to get the gist of it down quickly before he forgot.
It was another five hours before he took the bull by the horns and rung both his son and his eldest daughter. In his usual fashion, he decided that the best course of action was just to tell them the truth. So, first Matt, who would be home earlier, and then Tracey.
Each conversation followed the same pattern. Laughter. Disbelief. Was he taking the piss? (from his son), Was he OK? Could they talk to Gaynor? How was it possible?

139

Anything that they hadn't previously thought of. Then, "Dad, you really are serious, aren't you?"

"Never more so. I've spoken to her every day for a week and Gaynor and Ellie have talked to her too. It's been absolutely amazing."

Then the follow up questions. What does she look like? What did you talk about? How long would all this last? What happens when/if she goes? Why didn't he tell them earlier?

"Well you'll be able to ask her yourself as I've organised a Skype call. Can you both get to one house, later this evening?"

"No problem."

So Matt would go round to Tracey's and set up Skype while Tim would be taking the dog for a walk. Forty five minutes later, when Gaynor and Ellie got home, he got the call to say that they were ready. Fingers crossed. "Mum, you ready?"

If history had any independent assessment, this might well have been regarded as among the most surreal half hours, certainly in his family. Fortunately, it was just for them and undocumented. Unfortunately, and something he realised that only Gaynor and he noticed, but his mother wasn't quite her usual self. Indeed, she seemed a little faded and he feared the worst. She noticed his concern. "Michael, I'm OK but this is harder than I thought. The concentration on the screen is very tiring. I think I need to go. I'm very sorry to all of you. Can we meet again tomorrow, please?" And, with that, her image faded, both on and off the screen. Trying to make light of the situation, his response was,

"Well, same time tomorrow then?"

"Dad, has anything like this happened before?" It was Matt.

"No, nothing."

"So you don't know if it will be harder tomorrow?"

"No, I don't. She did say that she was OK and I took that

140

to mean that our time together isn't necessarily coming to an end. Why?"

"And she can't come up here?"
Now for two people who didn't always find conversation between one another as easy as they'd have liked, they were usually on the same wavelength. As they were this time.

"Well, Tracey is off work on Friday and, if Tim can get the MPV and gives me the day off, we can all come down. Didn't you say that what sustains your mum on her visits was the emotional power of you and her other close relatives? So, we'll come down and stay overnight. We can actually meet, in the flesh."

"Matt, hardly in the flesh." This was getting even more bizarre.

"But realistic, surely" That was Gaynor. "We can manage for one night."
And, in that even more surreal few minutes, it was decided. They'd be on their way, provided that the MPV was free. Well, it was and so would they be, the day after tomorrow. For quite a family gathering.
That night, as he and Gaynor lay in bed together, they tried to make sense of events over the last week or so.
"I just wanted to see my mum and talk to her. It seemed simple. Now we're having a family get together. I hope that it's not like some of the other ones that the Daligan family has had."

"That would be difficult, Mike. This is a Hudson family get together."
As usual, his wife brought a sense of perspective and humour to the situation and, for that, he was grateful.
"Sleep well. See you in the morning."

"You too."
The following morning he had the, now familiar, voice in his head and, he had to admit, that worried him.
"OK, Mum. I'm here."

She materialised and he saw straight away that she was just her usual self.

"Michael, you look worried. Try not to, it's OK. It just all got a bit much concentrating on that small screen."

"Sadly, it's what people do now much of the time."

"Why sadly? It's good to be able to talk like that and see who you're talking to, isn't it?"

"Yes, it is. What's not so good is, for a whole generation, technology seems to be the major means of communication of any sort. I prefer talking to actual people in real life. Then, again, I am getting older. Anyway, I have some news for you which I hope you'll like."

"Fire away, as your father would have said."

"Well, after last night, Tracey and Matt feel that, if you can't go to them, they'd like to come to you. Tomorrow evening, in fact. We'll have the family get together that we might have had in other circumstances. What do you think?"

"I think that's absolutely wonderful. Don't they have to work and how will they get here? It's a pity I can't travel as I've never been to Yorkshire. In fact, I've never been out of the Islands.

"Well, Tim has his own business and access to a big car. Matt is also self employed and Tracey has Friday's off. They're even going to bring the grandchildren. We'll all be together under one roof."
She looked beside herself with joy and couldn't stop the tears and neither could he.
This beat 'Long Lost Families' by miles. Eat your heart out, Davina.

"Do you want to come back this evening, Mum, when Gaynor and Ellie get home."

"Michael, if it's all the same with you, could I just sit here and watch television while you work?"

Now we're into 'Truly, Madly, Deeply' country.

So, for as long as they could sustain the visit, she watched 'Call the Midwife' and 'Upstairs, Downstairs'. He, like the dutiful son that he'd become, was 'her little man' again making sure that everything was alright. He'd waited years to be able to do that.

Eventually, they both realised that the visit was coming to an end.

"Give Gaynor and Ellie my love and my apologies and see you tomorrow."

"I will. Love you."

"Love you too, Michael."

Once she was gone, he texted his wife and youngest daughter to forewarn them. Then, with the need to get some fresh air, he spent the afternoon walking over the Heath. Cold, windy and fresh. Just what he needed. Now to get ready for when his family arrived.

A Larger Family
Gathering

It was very late when the tribe arrived and tribe it was. In addition to her youngest grandchild, there were his mother's two other grandchildren and three great grandchildren along with her eldest granddaughter's husband. This truly would be a momentous occasion. It was, in fact, the first time that they'd ever all been in the flat together even not counting his mother. He hoped that it wouldn't be a disappointment for any of them.

So by the time that their bags had been brought in and beds sorted out, it was 11.30 and too late to call her. Just as well as they were all tired and, anyway, the arrangement was for tomorrow. It was a bit of a squeeze with three of the men having to make do with folding beds in the living room. Still, it was only for one night, so needs must.

The following morning, the flat was abuzz with members of his family having to manage with the solitary bathroom and to step aside to let one another by. Breakfast, something he enjoyed cooking for all of them, was a bit of a conveyor belt. Whenever he watched cooking programmes, he'd always been amazed at how the chefs managed to cook for great numbers of people, while delivering all the courses when required. At the right temperature. And he only had nine breakfasts to prepare. Along with the requisite teas and coffees. Then there was all that washing up. Luckily he'd always found that task very therapeutic. Something that was useful given the circumstances. Finally, they were all settled down and could wait no longer.

"Don't forget to leave room for my mum to sit down. Budge up, Chris. All ready."
The anticipation was palpable.
"Mum, we're all here."
Quiet.
"Mum, are you there?"
Maybe it was his imagination but it seemed that there was a hesitancy. That her appearance wasn't as immediate as usual. But then, there she was looking extremely happy and, yes, apprehensive. He stood up and reached out.

"It's OK, Mum. It's only your family and we're all here."
She looked slightly taken aback by the fact that there were so many. Yes, he'd told her who they were but she hadn't quite expected this. Turning to the others, he said, "This is Lou, my mum." Before being overcome with emotion. It was her turn to put her arms around him. Holding hands, he turned back to the rest of his family to introduce them.

"Mum, Gaynor and Ellie, you know. Well this is Tracey, my eldest daughter and Matt, my son. This is Tim, Tracey's husband and these are Amy and Chris, their children. And this is the other Michael Daligan, Matt's son. They each reached out to her, some shyly and some without undue inhibition. It was quite an occasion for all of them.

"Do you mind if I sit down?" she said, "This all a bit overwhelming. Lovely, but more than I'd expected."
He moved over. "There you are, Mum," as she sat down.
For a moment nobody spoke until he heard, "You look too young to be my granny but I'm glad that you're here."
It was Tracey.
"Thank you, Tracey. You have to remember that you see me at the age I was when I died. That was over 70 years ago. Now, please, tell me about yourselves"
With the niceties out of the way, It was his mum who found

herself having to respond to just the questions that her son had asked her on their first meeting. About her life and that part of it with her son. What it was like in wartime London. Her mother and father, brothers and sisters. She, in turn, wanted to know all about them. Her death was never mentioned although the after-life was. Michael this time.

Without anyone realizing it, over two hours had passed, when Gaynor stood up to make the teas and coffees. "Don't worry, your granny doesn't eat or drink but that doesn't mean we can't."

She smiled, "Much as I'd like to join you."

He followed his wife as she walked towards the kitchen before going into the spare room to get his camera. He'd at least like to try to get a better likeness than he had, although anything that was taken would be kept strictly within the family. That had, after all, already been agreed as was the fact that today's get together wasn't to be mentioned to anyone else. At least while he was still alive. After that he'd have no control anyway. Having taken the shots that he thought would be good ones, he checked and, yes, the images were already fading. It seemed like his mother was right after all. Shame really but maybe just as well.

She looked over at him and smiled, "No luck."

"No."

"Michael, you need to remember, this is the embodiment of who I was and not the body of who I am."

"I know but I just thought I'd keep trying."

"You always did." And with that little throwaway line, she almost justified his whole approach to life. Something that he couldn't let pass.

"Thanks, Mum."

"You're welcome, my child."

Looking around him at all his immediate family, he was struck by how natural it felt to have them there, together under one roof. Then he remembered the dreams he'd had as a child of the head of a large family, while acknowledging that this, sometimes, felt uncomfortable. How that contrasted with his love of his own company and the other dreams that he'd had of travelling the world on his own. Something that really made him feel uneasy. This alongside the reality of upping sticks and moving when faced with emotionally difficult situations. It had taken a whole lifetime to make sense of these conflicting emotions and he still hadn't. Yet this seemed as close to it as he'd ever felt. So, a result of sorts and one that he could live with. He noticed too that the person whose absence he'd felt more than any other was at the centre of all this. And that pleased him enormously as it obviously did her. This the quiet one of her siblings, may have been an unlikely matriarch but there was no doubting the fact that she was at the centre of it all here.

"You OK, Dad?"

It was Matt. He smiled as he nodded. "Yeah, never better. You?"

"Amazing but you've got to admit it's weird. None of my comics have a plot like this one. And the difference is that this is real. It's happening. To us!"

They both laughed.

"I'm just pleased that she's got to meet her grandchildren and great grandchildren. Lots of people don't get to do that, especially the latter."

"Dad, most people don't have their granny come back from the dead!"

Again, big smiles from two who shared a very similar and, somewhat, odd sense of humour.

"Well, we need to make the best of it while we can."

"Dad, we've had something that we never imagined could happen so, when it ends, it'll be like the most amazing dream and something that will stay with us for the rest of our lives. So try to make sure that your mum leaves at a time when it's right for you. I'd hate for you to have a rerun of all those years ago."

"I know and thanks, son. The problem is that it's something that neither of us will have much control over. And, to be honest, I don't think now that it's too far away. Still, it is what it is and who would ever have expected that this would happen?"

147

"What are you two talking about? You look very serious."
It was Tracey this time.

"Just about how good this is but also how strange."

"Maybe we need to see if we can meet our other grand-mother. She didn't die as long ago but it was still just after I was born and before you, Matt."

"That's outside my province. You'd need to talk to your mum about that. But, you're right, this has been amazing. But, as I was explaining to your brother, I think that saying our final goodbyes isn't too far away."

"But we've only just met."

"It's not in our hands, my love. This is about my mum getting resolved and, she tells me, that's not a long process. Like I said to Matt, I think this might be a central part of that. She and I have had over a week together and now that she's met you all. Well, I just have a feeling."

"Have you asked her?"

"Yes, of course and that's what makes me feel this way. That and me feeling OK about it."

"OK? How can you be OK, Dad? Just when you've got to know her."

"Perhaps it's because I have finally got to know her. I've met the mother I never really knew and, yes, I'll be sad. But it won't be like last time. This time, I just feel that it will be as normal as these things can ever be. We'll all have been together and can say our goodbyes. Most importantly, it's what it will mean for her. She will rest in peace at last and I can visit her grave know-ing that I knew what she was like as a person. That, for me, is the most important part, grieving less so. After all, she actually died over 70 years ago. Mind you, all this is theory. I've no idea what I'll be like when she leaves for the last time."

148

"Talking of last times, Dad, does this have to be that for us or could we stay over again and say goodbye tomorrow before we leave?"

"Do you all want to stay as it'll be another squeeze?"

"I think Tim needs to get back but, if he goes by train, I can drive. I'll ask him."
And so it was agreed. They'd need to get back but proper goodbyes the following morning seemed to be the preferred option. Nobody, after all, wanted to leave someone they'd never see again. Anyway, they were enjoying themselves; the extended family that he'd always wanted revelling in each others' company. If this really did lead to resolution for his mum, she could scarcely have imagined that this would have been the setting.

As if to be reminded, he could hear her laughing and turned to see her surrounded by her grandchildren and great grandchildren who were listening to the antics that she and her siblings used to get up to when they were young. Different in many ways to their own experiences but similar in the relationship with her (and their) parents. She noticed him watching and smiled. In his work, he'd always tried to create what he called "little bits of Wonderland" for others, now his mum seemed to be living in hers. Although, he realised, perhaps living wasn't the most appropriate word. He also realised that, so far, he hadn't felt any tiredness. Was it the same for her and, if so, how long would that continue to be the case? He thought that he'd best ask and walked over to where she was talking.

"Now, you lot, I know you're enjoying yourselves but do you lot mind if I get five minutes with my mum, please?"
They walked into the garden that she'd been so taken with when he first showed her round.

"A bit bigger than the one we had at Edale Road" as she'd described it.

"I know what you're going to say, Michael, and, yes, the tiredness is starting to catch up in a way that it hadn't only yesterday. It's as if I've been buoyed up by the combined emotion of all of you and, as a result, might be more tired afterwards."

"I did wonder. So, why don't we go back inside and I'll just explain. You can then sit down and enjoy the surroundings so that, when you do feel, you can't sustain it any longer, they'll be ready. Now that they're staying overnight again, there's the opportunity to put off saying goodbye until tomorrow. Then we can Skype or whatever once they're back home."

She beamed, "Of course, I'd forgotten. I wish we'd had all this years ago. Who knows what would have happened between Dorrie and me then."

He didn't want to say that the technology and medical advances might also have given her a longer life. There seemed no point.

"What have you two been hatching up?"

It was Gaynor. Quietly he said, "Just talking about timing, my love, just in case."

Then to everyone else, "Listen my mum's been here a lot longer than normal (if normal was the right word) and she's starting to feel a little tired. If she gets any more so, she might not be able to stay here for much longer. So, if it's OK, she's going to sit quietly. Don't worry, though, she'll be back tomorrow. Tea, coffee and cake, anyone?"

While he brewed up and cut the cake, he was careful to watch. She did look tired but she also looked like someone in her element. It's just a pity that refreshments were beyond her as that would have made the perfect end to the visit. Still, "C'est la vie."

Sitting down with their tea and cake, his mother asked, "Would any of you mind if I watched something on the television."

It hadn't occurred to any of them.

"How about an old film, Granny. I'm sure we could find something for you."

Perhaps not a war film.

They settled on 'Hobson's Choice'. Set in the period a generation before she was born, it featured Charles Laughton, long one of his favourite actors. It was, it turned out a film she thoroughly enjoyed although the younger generation soon found their laptops and tablets more interesting and adjourned to Ellie's room. The timing couldn't have been better and, a little after the film ended, so did her visit. Huge hugs all round and a few tears.

"See you in the morning."

"See you tomorrow, Lou/Mum/Granny."

And, with that, the room and a large part of their lives felt empty.

The Morning After

The following morning, a little bleary eyed, they sat down to breakfast. Although not the noisy fry up that they'd shared the day before. This was a rather more subdued occasion; not all of that explained by the alcohol that had been consumed. Looming over most of them was the fact that this morning would see them say their goodbyes. At least in person. Understandably, perhaps, the subject was avoided; another elephant in the room in what was already a rather crowded flat. Perhaps that's why, with the washing up done, he adjourned to the garden. It, after all, had room for an elephant.

He hadn't been out there long, lost in thought, when his youngest daughter joined him, along with his coat. "Thought you might need this, Dad. What time are you going to call her?"

"I'm not sure. Not too late as they all have to get home and it's a long drive. I was rather putting it off."

"I just spoke to Tracey and she says that they need to get away soon as they all need to be up for work in the morning.

"I guess I need to call her then but what do we say to her? I've never had to do anything like this before."

"Dad, neither has anyone else. Saying goodbye to a ghost isn't something that you do every day of the week, Just call her and we'll take it from there."

"OK, although I might suggest another Skype call when they get back. That way this isn't a dramatic final goodbye; more a sort of au revoir. Yes, it will be difficult when they get back but they'll already be 200 miles away by then. It's goodbye in easy stages, if you like."
Ellie squeezed his hand. This didn't seem the time to remind him about his own farewell to her in the not too distant future.
They looked up to see Tracey and Gaynor coming out to join them. They'd obviously been talking and bore the look that he knew so well; that of dealing with whatever they had to while trying to reassure everyone else that it would be OK. Now how did he know that that would be the case with all these women? It was Gaynor who spoke. Putting her arms around him, she said, "Mike, they do need to say goodbye to your mum."

"I know. It's just that I don't know how to go about it."

"You don't have to just yet, but they do."

"OK, I'll call her and then we can Skype when you get home."

"I like that. I'll ring you as soon as we do."
They went into the house where the rest of the family was gathered.
"I'm going to call my mum so that you can say goodbye in person. Then we can do a Skype call when you get back, if that's OK?"

And, with that, he called.

She was there almost immediately, smiling and a little uneasy. She too had had time to think about the situation and to discuss it with the others. She also had that "calm, despite everything" look. Then he realised that all his family looked like that, except him. Once again, he was the exception and not the rule. You'd have thought that he'd have got used to it by now but, no, he hadn't. Perhaps if he took a step back and let them get on with it in their own way? So, having explained to his mum when they needed to leave and what was planned for this evening, that's exactly what he did.

What started out tentatively with none of them wanting to say anything untoward soon became the 'sad but happy' occasion that he'd hope that it would be. Sad that goodbyes were being said but happy that they'd had the chance to meet his mum and now had an actual memory of her. It was about half an an hour later that his mother looked over towards him.

"Michael, this is making me more tired than I'd imagined and I'm not sure that I can hold on much longer. I'm sorry but I need to say goodbye to you all. "

What followed were slightly hurried but, nonetheless, deeply felt farewells. It would be fair to say that no one was dry eyed. Then she wasn't there anymore.

"I think I'll put the kettle on." It was his usual response to difficult personal situations and it was to be so this time. While the rest of his family sat in the living room with their own thoughts, he busied himself with teas and coffees. And, even when these had been made, little was said. Finally, Tracey stood up.

"Dad, I think, maybe, it's time we got on the road. Will you be OK?"

He got to his feet and hugged her, "Yeah. You have a safe journey. Shall I make you some sandwiches?"

"No, that's OK, we've got to fill up so we'll get some then."

"Are you sure? It's no problem."

"No, we'll get going if that's OK?"

More hugs as he walked them to the front door then to the car. As they were about to drive off, he felt that insistence in his head again.

"Mum?"

Michael, it's OK, I'm watching. I just thought it might be easier this way. Give them a hug from me and tell them I'll speak to them on the computer tonight.

"You OK, Dad?"

"I'm fine, Matt. I'll speak to you tonight. Love you." And, with that, he shut the passenger door and waved as they drove away. The last thing he, Gaynor, Ellie and his mother saw was the grandchildren waving out of the back window. They got back into the house to his mother's voice.

Michael, call me.

No sooner had he done so than a very sad but happy mother appeared. "I'm sorry, my child, but it was getting a bit over-whelming and I thought that that was the best way. Not too much fuss."

"I never realised that ghosts could fake it as well as those who're alive."

"So, you've learnt something new today, then. Anyway, I really am tired so, if you don't mind I'll see you later. Don't worry, I feel fine."

"Granny."

It was Ellie. "I love you." This with a tight embrace. "Will I see you later as well?"

"Of course you will."

And with that and a big smile on her face, she was gone.

A Skype Farewell

Early that evening the phone rang. It was Tracey to say that they'd got home safely although the journey had taken a little longer than they'd expected. How were they all?

"We're fine, thank you, my love. It's just that it's all been a bit of a blur since you left."

"Is your mum OK and can we still talk this evening?"

"Yes and yes. I'll ring her as soon as you're ready."

"Well we're having a takeout this evening, Dad, so I'll ring you when we've eaten. Probably about an hour?"

"Are Matt and Michael eating with you?"

"An Indian? What do you think?"

"OK. Ring you at about seven."
The next hour passed very slowly. Finally, at 7.30, he called his mother. The person who appeared seemed more at ease than he did. If he didn't know better, he might have felt that she was coming to terms with the eventual outcome.

Then, again, perhaps he didn't know better and she actually was. If that was the case, he felt glad for her and hoped that he could face the future just as well. One thing at a time, though. They needed to get this one out of the way first. And, with that, he put the call through.

It was Matt who answered. He was in Tracey's living room and had connected the large TV up to the laptop so that they could all get in front of the screen easier. Even Bailey, the dog, was in shot. He, Gaynor and Ellie were sat in front of the desktop. The expressions on both screens ranged from stoicism, through worry and concern, to inevitable acceptance. OK, now to call her. She came through smiling although, obviously, looking as apprehensive as everyone else.

"Hello, Mum. As you can see, we're all here."

"Even the dog", she noted. "Well, it's lovely to see you all, the family that, until two days ago, I'd never met." Her voice went quiet as she stopped. "You have to excuse me" she stopped again, "all the years of waiting hadn't prepared me for this. Unfortunately, the yearning gets to be a habit, you get used to it. The strength of the feeling doesn't really get any less but knowing what actual feelings are like, does. Maybe it's strong because of why I'm here now. With you all" Again, she stopped. He reached out to hold her hand. Her little man again, trying to make it better for his mum. She smiled at him. "It's alright, Michael. It's not like last time and, although I'd love to stay, I know that my time here is near its end. Funny, but I don't feel too bad about that. I just need to try to make sure that you, my family, feel the same." She looked at the screen and smiled at them all. Sad but happy at the same time. They were all quiet, as if there were no words. Which, in truth, there weren't. Still, he felt the need to say something.

"Mum, I think we all feel the same. We'd sooner that this wasn't happening but it is and we all want you to feel as easy about it as you can. It's important that this works for you. You've waited for it for so long."

"It's alright, Michael, you need to remember that I've

been to funerals and said goodbye to my father, my sister Lally and quite a few others, lots of who, like me, died young. From the little I've learned, that's not so common now. So, it's all of you I'm worried about."

There were smiles at the thought that they were all trying to make it better for someone whose sole aim was to make it better for them.

"Mum, I just want it to be alright!"

There he'd said it. The cry of a small child echoing down the years from a lifetime ago.

She reached out and held his hand. "It's alright, my child. Live the rest of your life with your family and remember that I loved you. You were my sunshine, not your father."

He allowed it all to wash over him taking him to somewhere that he'd forgotten existed. A time when a young woman and her small child were as one, happy just being together. Years of hurt and worry taken away, to be replaced by the love they felt for one another. A love they were now both able to enjoy, albeit for a very short time. She pulled him closer so that they were oblivious to the rest of the world. Oblivious, even to the rest of his family. Until, that is, he felt two other pairs of arms around him and realised that he was being held by three of the most important people in his life and watched by the others. To say he felt a strong feeling of ease deep inside would be an understatement. It was contentment personified.

Michael, are you watching this?

As they let go of one another, it was his mother who started to speak. "I want you all to know that this has all been better than I could ever have imagined. And, as you might have thought, I've imagined it many times over the years. I thought about Michael most of the time; that never really went away. And I hoped that one day he'd call and we would meet. Well, my child, eventually you did and it was well worth the wait. Seeing you, hearing about your life and meeting your family, well, it's been more than I could ever have dreamt of. Meeting all my grandchildren and great grandchildren has been something special. I knew that I had at least one grandchild but to see two more and then three great grandchildren, well, it was the icing on the cake. To see that little boy I left all those years ago in the midst of you all will remain with me for as long as, well, as long as I've still got." She smiled as she looked at the screen.

There was still no comment from those watching via the desktop. It was almost as if they were in an episode of "The Waltons" only considerably less schmaltzy. Broad smiles and, from his children, the enjoyment of watching their father as happy as they'd ever seen him. For those who'd been there when he was at his lowest, this was a real blessing.

Sometimes within families, there is a collective antenna when what isn't being said registers with them all and this was one such time. Moreover, it was picked up by someone who, in his younger days, had been singularly lacking in the necessary empathy to do just that.

"Mum, all of you, I'm not sure that anything could top this. Like you, Mum, it's something that I'd dreamt about but never thought would happen. How could it, you weren't alive? Well, it has and it has been the most amazing experience. I really did have a mother and, what's more, she's here to prove it. If I was a religious person (smiles all round), I'd say that truly there is a god. However, this is also a very sad time because mum isn't likely to be around much longer. Like the rest of us she doesn't really want to go but knows that she must. From what I've read, when people have a painful, terminal illness, needing the pain to go away eventually becomes stronger than the will to stay. I guess this is similar." His mother nodded.

"So, I think what I'm trying to say is that we're reliant on you to let us know when that is."

She looked very sad, "Michael, yes, I know that I haven't much longer and need to make the most of the strength that I have left. That's what makes it difficult. I want to spend as much time with you all as I can but…" She stopped, hesitating, then continued, "Most importantly, Michael, I need the strength to say a proper goodbye to you this time." She looked at the screen and said, "I'm sorry."

It was as if the sound had been turned down until Matt spoke. "It's OK, Granny, you and Dad need that time. We've had time with you, time that we'd never thought

159

possible. So, if you need to say goodbye, we can do that. I have the chance now to tell my grandchildren and, maybe, great grandchildren, that I met my grandmother. I can also tell them what she was like."

"I like that. So, if it needs to be goodbye then so be it." You could always rely on Matt to say what needed to be said. She looked at the screen to see that they were all nodding despite holding back their tears.

"One thing, Granny," it was Matt again. "If you find that you do feel strong enough, just get dad to give us a call. That would be great."

"I will do." The reluctance to say those final words was palpable. The reluctance to hear them, just as much. Then looking at each in turn, "Love you all, Tracey, Matt, Amy, Chris, Michael, Tim and, of course" she smiled, "Bailey."
"God bless and have long and happy lives. And remember your granny. The one you all helped to find peace. Thank you." There was silence but they all still sat where they were in front of the screen reluctant to leave the room. Again, it was Matt who walked up and looked directly at his grandmother. They were both crying, "Granny, I love you and thanks for giving us dad. And for making his life complete. When we get down to London, we'll visit with flowers."

"White roses, please, Matt, always my favourites."
He nodded and looked at all the others who did the same. Then he looked back at those in London and, saying, "Goodbye", turned the computer off.
Perhaps it was just as well that those in each location couldn't see the others, as what they would have witnessed was sadness and grief at both locations. None of them would sleep too soundly that night. An hour or so later he got his first call from Tracey to see if he was alright and, later, after the pub had closed, one from Matt. They were much appreciated.

The Anniversary

Throughout his adult life, he'd occasionally had thoughts about being elsewhere to where (and when) he was now. In his case, it was a very specific time and place. Harrogate during the summer of 1977. He'd moved there with his eldest children the year before to start a new life and, as spring changed to summer, he felt free for the first time in his life. He could describe the feeling for that time as a yearning, a longing, but those words wouldn't convey the depth of the emotion. Even "hunger" didn't do it. On those days, it was as if he really had to turn the clock back and actually BE THERE. Perhaps it was no surprise then that the feeling returned on the day after his family had gone home and he was nearing the time to say the most important goodbye of his life. This, too, he realised would become one of those times and places that that feeling would return to him. Perhaps unsurprisingly, it was something that he quite looked forward to experiencing over the years. Now to call his mother. It wasn't long before she stood in front of him. She, too, looked a little circumspect.

"Hello, Mum."

"Hello, my child."

"You OK?"

"I think so. I'm still recovering. When you told me that I would meet them all, I just thought that it would be nice. I didn't expect that. It made me very sad as I realised what I'd missed all those years. It also made me happy, inside, to know that I'd left something behind. A little bit of me."

"It looked quite a big bit to me, Mum. Certainly they'll never forget their grandmother."

"Or great grandmother."

"If you had more time, it might even be great, great grandmother."

"One great is enough, thank you. After all, it's the most I could have expected in life."
Without realizing it, she'd given him as good a time as any to talk about the elephant in the room.

"You don't feel tired from yesterday then?"

"I wouldn't go so far as to say that, my child. After all it was a long while for an unresolved to stay around. Pretty unique, I understand, to harness all that emotion and for so long. In fact, nobody had actually heard of a family gathering before."

"Isn't it commonsense?"

"It doesn't seem as though it was and anyway, from what I've gathered, you have a fairly unusual idea of what commonsense is."
Although "Ouch" came out of his mouth, he couldn't help but smile.
"Are you tired, Michael?"

"Now that they've all gone back home I am. It's like it's catching up on me." He almost said jetlag but didn't really want to have to explain something else about modern life to her. What he did have to say was more important.

"Mum, can we talk?"

"I thought we were already doing that"

"Yes but not about, well, about how much longer we might have together."
There, said it!
"I wondered when you might bring that up again. Is there a reason?"

"Maybe. You see I feel that having the whole family together seems to have changed things, for you more than me."

"It's funny but even as a small child you were very susceptible to my emotions, my feelings and you seem to have carried that into your adult like."
His heart sank. "So things have changed?"
"Well, I do feel different. Only a little, maybe but, yes."
This isn't getting any better.

"From what I know, each unresolved who's gone through this has sorted out what was causing them to be that way in the first place. So, naturally, I assumed that that would be what decided when the end came. When, in fact, I would be released from limbo."

"And it isn't?"
Please say that I have some influence.
"I don't know but I thought that it would be just the feeling getter weaker as I grew easier with what had happened all those years ago. Now I think that that might not be all of it. Seeing all of you over the last few days seems to have made it easier for me to let go. It's not that I don't feel strong. Quite the opposite. I do feel strong, strong enough to say goodbye. I'm so sorry, Michael. I thought that it would be entirely out of my hands but, in reality, me making the decision might be what helps me to be at peace."

She looked up through tears to see that he, too, was crying.

"Mum, I can't let you go. I'm not ready to say goodbye. Not yet. Can't we talk?"

"Of course we can. You know that I'm not saying goodbye now but just trying to explain."

"You do know what day this is don't you?"

"Michael, how could I not? Today is the anniversary of my funeral. And I'm still here. It seems that we may have managed to get beyond what was expected."

"Do you think that that may have something to do with the length of time you waited and the strong desire that that created?"

"Who knows? It's funny but I do feel more in control so, let's just enjoy what we have, especially this anniversary, a milestone that I didn't expect to see."

"Me neither. At least not in this way."

"So, you thought that this would be our last day?"

"Yes, I suppose I did. Also, such anniversaries get more important as the length of time in limbo gets longer and the chances of being resolved get less."

"Is that why I heard your voice in my head and why it got louder until I responded?"

"Yes, I think so."

"So that helped bring us together and now, having the whole family together helps you to stop being a ghost. To rest in peace."

"It would seem so."

"Sounds like euthanasia for the dead."

Stupid, bloody stupid. Why did he have to say that?

"Michael, what's euthanasia?"

Now it gets bloody worse. Idiot.

"It's when human beings are terminally ill and they get the chance to end their own lives voluntarily. Not in England but people do travel overseas with their loved ones to enable them to do it at a time of their own choosing."

"To commit suicide. Michael, that's wrong. Don't they know that?"

"Mum, it's a choice if people are dying. I'd do it if I was in that situation."

"Like I was, you mean?"

Mike, when you're in a hole, stop digging.

"Mum, this is a silly time to have a disagreement, so...."

"You're right, my child. It is. So, let's start again, shall we? I know, why don't you read some more to me? I'd like that. We must be getting near the end of the story."

"Well, we've still a way to go so how about I jump a little to the part where I meet Gaynor and my life starts to get much better."

"That would be nice. Then, perhaps, I could watch a little television?"

"Of course, Mum. I have some work to do anyway if that's OK?"

"Give me a minute while I make a cuppa."

Putting the kettle on, he looked over into the living room to see that she was looking through his book at the photos. And smiling. Walking through with his tea in his hand, he sat down.

Opening the book, he said, "OK, I meet Gaynor. Here we go."

She sat quietly while he read. Until, that is, he got to the part where they were on holiday in France when Ellie, then about seven years of age, decided to light a candle in a church they visited. When he read the part where she'd told him that that was for his mum, she was unable to hold back the tears. Eventually, getting to the chapter in which his wife decided to become a teacher, he stopped.

"I think that's enough for today and leaves us with just a little more before we get to the end. I call that 'Mike's Story'. It's the counterpoint to 'Michael's Story' at the beginning. TV, Mum?"

"That would be nice. What is there?"

"She settled for another episode of 'Call the Midwife' while he sat at the computer, writing. An older person in the company of a younger person, two people obviously enjoying one another's company, in a scene that was probably repeating itself in many other areas of the country. Except, of course, with an unusual twist. Even when they turned the television off and he, having made himself a cup of tea, sat down on the sofa next to her. It still looked similar. Except that the conversation now seemed to have turned to something more serious. Which it had.

"So, Mum, where do we go from here?"

"I'm not sure, Michael, I was hoping that you might have some thoughts. After all, from what you've read to me, you've often had to get yourself out of difficult situations. And, what's more, you've usually succeeded, haven't you?"

"I guess so but there's a difference between working out how to rescue an organisation and make it successful and getting through extremely difficult personal situations."

"But you've done both."

"Yes, I have. The difference is that, with the personal ones, I didn't think about it, I just got through it. I don't want to 'just get through' this one. This is you and me saying our goodbyes. Forever." The definiteness of his voice, as usual, disguising the apprehensiveness he felt underneath.

"Michael, this isn't like last time, you know. Now we have some control. Last time I was too ill to care and you were too young to know."

"Yes, I was but I knew that something bad was about to happen to you and I was very scared."
It's OK, little man, I'm here. Don't worry.
I'm frightened. Will it be alright?
Yes. I told you, I'm here. I'm not going anywhere.
OK.
He wondered what thoughts were going through his mother's head and sensed that she was trying not to show her feelings too much. Not showing his feelings was something that didn't come easy to him. Although, to be fair, maybe it was the same for her and she was just trying harder.

"Well what we do know is that we've probably not get very long but that we don't know precisely when. So, let's ignore when and look at how. That way we can make plans and be ready whenever it is."

"You've done this before, haven't you?"
He smiled, "Someone did it for me once when I was in a similar situation and it helped enormously."
"What happened?"

"It was Dan, my therapist when we were talking about ending it and I was aware that that meant that I probably wouldn't ever see him again. That made me very concerned, made worse by the fact that I had no idea how to say goodbye. Dan then asked me what I wanted to say. So I told him that I wanted to say how important he'd been, how much he'd helped change my life, how I felt about him and to say goodbye by shaking his hand. His response was, apart from the handshake, hadn't I just done that. At which point, I cried. He was a wily old bird who, I think, became the father figure I never had."
She looked straight at him, "So, what do you want to tell me, my child?"

He smiled. "I think you know that, don't you, Mum?"

"It would be nice to hear it."

He looked down, "I think I'd want to say that the most important thing is that I've found out that you were a real person and that I spent time with just like any other child did with their mother. That was really important to me."

He looked up at her to see that she had a smile on her face.

"Anything else?"

"That I've realised that you fought ill health for five years so that you could be there for me. You didn't just give up."

"I would never have done that to you, Michael, you must know that."

"I do now but I don't think I did then. Otherwise I wouldn't have these feelings. You were there with me, then you got that letter from my father and then you were gone." He looked towards her again to see that she was looking hurt. "It's hard for me to hear that's how you felt because you were the most important person in my life."

"Mum, I'm not blaming you. You didn't cause it, he did. And, if he'd behaved differently, you and me might have had more time together. I would have known you."

Wistfully, she asked, "Do you know me now, my child?"

He could feel his face break into a broad grin as he replied, quietly, "I think so."

"And."

"I like the person that you are."

"Not love, then?"

"Yes, of course although I don't find that easy to say."

"Why's that?"

"Because, when I loved you before, you died."

There, he'd said it. A lifetime of pent up feeling released in one

168

short outburst.

She moved towards him and put her arms around him. First gently and then with some urgency. It was as if a dam had burst inside him but one in which the contents were now contained by her embrace. He was that child again; the one before he became the little man that she needed him to be. Now the roles were reversed and all was as it should be. Now their final goodbye would be no less sad, although it would be with nothing left unsaid and, perhaps, that's as much as anyone could ask.

It was his mother who broke the silence, "Michael, would it be alright if we said goodbye for now and you call me later? I just feel tired and need time to think."

"Is that because of what day it is?

"Probably. Certainly my feelings are more up and down as I think about what happened."

"You and me both. Same time?"

"Whatever's good for you, my child. Love you."

"Love you too, Mum." Those words, uttered as she faded away, had never sounded more apposite in his head. What he didn't tell her was that he'd recently had another email from Southwark Council. This one to say that the area around her grave had finally been cleared and a small cross placed on the plot to confirm that this was where she was buried. Now he could visit it knowing that, before too long, she would be there, finally, at peace. Which is why, with her unexpectedly early departure, he set off for the cemetery with a garden trowel and an old vase in his backpack. He hoped that Doll had been right, all those years ago, about what flowers his mum liked then he remembered that she'd mentioned it to Matt when they'd been talking.

Nunhead Cemetery had always been a special place ever since that first visit over thirty years ago. It seemed to him that it looked and felt like the Victorian cemetery that it was. A place where death, rather than being hidden away, was acknowledged, even celebrated. Where those who were permanent residents gradually being reclaimed by nature in much the same way that the cemetery itself was. This "managed decay" being an official recognition of the ultimate power of nature to prevail over human endeavour. Moreover, it contained catacombs, designed so that those remaining could commune with the relatives and friends who had "departed". That November morning the chill and mist also served to emphasise both the condition of those interred and the veil that they'd passed through en route. Fortunately, it didn't reflect his state of mind.

It was a mere five minute walk from the station to the cemetery gates. From there, up the slight incline, could be seen the ruined chapel that would still have been in use on that other November morning. Once at the top, there was a view over the city itself. The path to the right took him up another incline until he reached a fork from which the left hand path took him down to the grave. The cross was still in place marking the spot where the headstone would be placed next year.

With the flowers still in his hand, he cut across the grass to grave number 42047. As had been the case on his last visit, standing over where she lay, gave him a feeling of being totally at peace. It was as near to her as he'd ever been since she was laid out in the front room at Edale Road and it left him as relaxed as he'd ever felt.

"Hello, Mum, it's only me. Just brought you some flowers. Aunt Doll told me that these were your favourites, so I hope you like them and that I don't disturb you too much."

With that, he took the trowel out of his backpack and dug a small, cylindrical hole to accommodate the vase. Once that was in place, he filled it with some water that he'd drawn from a nearby tap, and dropped the flowers in with just a little rearrangement. His task completed, he put the backpack down and sat on it. Yes, it may have been cold but this was a time to savour and something that he wanted to be able to repeat whenever he felt the need to in the years ahead. After all, it had taken him a while to get around to it. With his mother not being as present as she was at home, he felt slightly more free in his one way conversation. Made easier by the fact that it was only in his head.

Mum, I'm not sure what to say that I haven't already said. Except that I did love you and now I know that you loved me. You, my mum, a real person and not just someone else who was absent from my life. That, before I became your little man, I was also your child and, listen to this, I still am. I belonged to some-one, Ada Louisa Hudson and that I have just as much of you in me as I have of my father. Feeling that has been a revelation to me. As has realising that we had time together when we were both happy.

I'm still angry that no one in my father's family ever talked about you. So I couldn't either. Just the mention of your name would have made all the difference. I'm also sorry that my only way of coping was to eradicate you from my life; to pretend that you'd never existed in the first place. That locked everything about you away. Yes, your dying scarred me beyond anything I could have imagined but that pretending also shut out the good times. As a small child, I may well not have remembered any of them but those memories would have been there inside me. What a differ-ence that would have made to my life. Happy memories of you and me together! Well, I have feelings about those now and that, too, feels good.

The other thing, that I don't know if I've told you, is that we plan to put up a headstone so that other people will know who you were. And, when my times comes, I want some of my ashes scattered over your grave and my name added to yours. My search will have come to an end. Yes, I will "rage against the dying of the light" but I will do so in the knowledge that, at least, I'd finally joined up all the bits.

He could hold back the tears no longer and, if anyone saw him, so what? He doubted that those visiting a grave did so in the lightest of moods so he wouldn't be out of place cry-ing. He did, though, take the trouble to look around and saw that those he could see had other things on their mind than watching an old man with tears running down his face. Tears that, to a degree, belied the ease he felt within. Now for the journey home where he hoped that his mum had had the rest she needed.

An hour and a half later and he was in the house thankful that he'd left the heating on. It was still only three o'clock and time for a sandwich before he called.

"Mum, are you feeling alright? It would be good to talk."

"Hello, my son. Yes, not too bad considering the circumstances. You've been out somewhere?"

"You know I have. I went to the cemetery to put some flowers on your grave.

"White roses I see."

"So, you saw me?"

"Yes. I sensed you were there so I watched. And listened. Did you think that I wouldn't?" She smiled.

"I hoped you would although I wasn't quite sure if you'd be in spirit or like we are now."

"Like I said, I could but I would have looked out of place and, anyway, you needed the time to yourself, didn't you?" He nodded. "It was nice although a little sad. Still we're both here now."

"It was nice to hear you say what you did. Most mothers would like their sons to talk about them like that even if it was painful to hear bits of it."

"I've waited a long time to be able to say what I did." She laughed. "And I've waited even longer to hear it." At that, he looked down aware of what he wanted to say but apprehensive about saying it.

"Michael, we both know what we need to talk about."

"Is it near the end?"

"Yes, I think so. The anniversary of the funeral exerts quite a pull from beyond and, although I can still hold on, it has taken more out of me to stay here."

"I hadn't noticed. How can that be?"

172

"I've tried hard to make sure that you didn't but right now, I can't ignore it much longer."

"How long?"

"I'm not sure but what I do know is that I don't want to be dragged to somewhere I've never been. I'd like to be in control of what will happen so that I can cope with it better. Isn't that a bit like, what did you call it, voluntary euthanasia?"
That'll teach you to be so free and easy with your comments.
"When?" One word that was more loaded with significance than any other that he'd ever uttered.
She looked at him with tears in her eyes and a look that was both sad and resolute. "I thought tomorrow might be best. That'll be after the anniversary and I don't think that I could be sure of any more time together."
"Mum, I can't. I just can't. It's too soon."

"Michael, I feel as though we may not have a choice and didn't you once tell me that, when it came to saying goodbye, you'd always found it easier to just get on with it?"

"Mum, I never allowed for this. I'll never see you again, ever."

"I'm sure we'll meet again when it's your turn to come after me. In the meantime, I'll always be here", pointing to his heart. As she did so he reached out and grabbed her hand, pulling her towards him. He felt her arms around him and then, from deep inside, a great well of sadness, then despair. He was that small child again only, this time, he knew just what was happening and, again, he could do nothing to prevent it. They stayed like that for some minutes with him crying. Until, eventually, she allowed her arms to drop until she was just holding his hands.
"I've always loved you, my child. You're what kept me going when I had nothing else and now you have to let me go. I don't want it anymore than you do but I want our parting to be as agreeable as it's possible for it to be. For both of

us. I can't take the risk that it might be like my first death was. We both deserve better than that."

"Mum, my head tells me that you're right but this hurts. Yes, if it has to be, I'll support you in your departure. I just need some time to get my head around it. After all, you will just cease to exist and I'll still be here dealing with the aftermath. I need to feel that I can. I know I have my family but you're my mum and you only get one of those. So, can I have some time to think, please?"

"Of course. Do you want me to leave you for a while and you call me when you're ready? Is that OK?"

"I don't really want to let you out of my sight but, yes, I think I'd like that."

"Call me when you're ready but not too long. I don't want to let you go either."
She smiled sadly and kissed him before she disappeared and he was left alone with his thoughts and they weren't happy ones. Inside, the feelings that were little Michael's started to reassert themselves so the first thing that he had to do was to calm those childlike emotions down. Something he'd been doing for more years than he cared to remember. Then he started to work on his own.
Mike, you know that you have no choice in this. It's really her decision.
I know, like I said, I just need some time.
OK. You wanna talk?
That's what we're doing ain't it
OK, OK. Just trying to help.
Well, you're not.
I'll shut up then.
You do that. It'll make a change.

There was silence which didn't make it any better. Eventually.

OK, we can talk if you want to.

174

I'd just like to help.
I know. Sorry.
You don't need to be, this is about as shitty as it gets.
You can say that again.
I could but I'm not going to. What you gonna do?
Like you said, I have no choice and, anyway, I want to make it as easy as possible for her to make the decision.
You know she already has.
Yep and that's hard for me. Although, in an odd way, it makes it easier dealing with a decision that's already been taken.
The story of your childhood.
He smiled to himself.
I'm so glad that I got the chance to know her.
That's pretty obvious.
Is it?
Look at yourself. Underneath the pain, you have an ease that most people never get.
She loves you, Mike, and you love her and it shows.
Without realising it, he had his arms around himself and he was crying. Also without realising it, he was calling out to her. Not intending for her to turn up but just calling her name. And there she was. She put her arms around him and held him tightly. A mother trying to ease her child's pain as mothers have done since time immemorial. He felt her hand on his shoulders, stroking him. All the while he heard, "Shush, my child. I'm here. We'll be alright." Again, like all those mothers, it wasn't necessarily so but it helped. Just as it had always done. Even if he'd forgotten that. Eventually they let go of one another and just took pleasure in what was in front of them. Two people for whom the richness of what is probably the most crucial relationship in life, was cut so short.

Michael, just enjoy it for what it is now and make sure that your mum does. When it's all over, you'll still have had this and how many people can say that?
Yes, I know and I will. And, if a little bit more hurt helps her to rest in peace, well, so be it.
You see, you're really quite a good person, after all.
He smiled at that thought and, with it, the realisation that his mother would never have thought it to be otherwise.

You always were a smartarse but I guess we can both live with that.

Amen to that, my boy. Now I'm off. You just enjoy the time that you have left and, if you need me again, just text "smartarse"! See you.

You too. And thanks.

Then it all went quiet in his head and he was left with the thought of that final parting.

"Mum."

"Michael"

"No, you first."

"OK", she said before she hesitated, "I think we both know what we need to talk about, don't we?"

He nodded, feeling easier about it than he had been just a few minutes ago. "Somehow, knowing how we were for most of the time we had together, makes an enormous difference. Now, I'll have that with me for the rest of my life and it's difficult to describe just how good that feels. Up until now, I thought that the sadness at the end was how it had always been. I'm sorry, Mum, but it overshadowed everything for me."

"I'm sorry too, Michael. I was so distraught when I read that letter that I couldn't cope and you got caught up in the aftermath. It wasn't fair. "

He smiled, "It's OK, Mum, now it really is water under the bridge. You have nothing to be regretful for and I have a great deal to feel good about. Yes, I'll be sad but sad with good memories. Memories of you. After all these years you won't be the only one at peace".

He looked at her to see that she had the most enormous smile on her face. A smile that brought back childhood memories of those better times. At which he, too, broke into a big grin.

"OK ", he said, "Let's part on memories of the good and not the sad. Let me talk to Gaynor and Ellie as I'm sure they'll want to talk to you and then we can, well, you know what."

"You do that and then, yes, we can. Now, have you got some writing to do as I'd like to watch a bit of television, if that's alright."

Glad that they were doing normal things at the end, he switched the set on. "Mum, you won't have seen "Passport to Pimlico" will you?"

That proved to be the end of his writing for the time being as they settled on the sofa together. He with a cup of tea and her rather wishing that she could drink one. An hour and a half later and it was time for her to leave.

"Call me later, Michael, when Gaynor and Ellie get home."

"I will. Don't worry. I love you, Mum."
There, that wasn't so hard, was it?
You still around?
Of course. Why not?
I'm busy right now. So off you go.
OK. See ya.

"I love you too, my son. See you later."

And, with a sad expression on her face, she was gone and the final goodbye drew nearer.

The End Draws Near

Two hours later, with supper prepared, he heard the key in the lock and Gaynor came through the door and, half an hour after that, Ellie followed.

"What's for supper, Dad, I'm hungry."

"I've done pasta bake. Hope that's OK?"
They chatted over the meal. Nothing of great import, despite the elephant in the room. In fact, probably because of it. Finally, he decided to broach the subject and, as usual, came straight to the point.

"You know Mum and I have been talking over the past two days about saying our goodbyes? Well, for all our sakes, we've decided that we don't want it to be forced on us by circumstance. That would be like her original death all over again. So, we would rather not drag it out."
His youngest daughter was taken aback, hurt even.

"Dad, don't we get any say in this?"

"I'm sorry, my love, but it's what your granny wants and

I agree with her. She knows that it's very near the end anyway and she wants to be able to say goodbye properly before something happens that might drag her away."

"Is that what will happen?"

"From what she's learned, yes, and probably quite quickly once she gets to that stage. Also, for some reason, the anniversary of her death creates an imperative to get her here, so the anniversary of the funeral can have the opposite effect."

"Dad, have you only just found that out?"

"Well, she did say something when she first appeared but I didn't pick up on it. It didn't seem right to push it and, since then, well, it felt awkward."
There was an uncomfortable silence while they both took this in and while he felt that he'd let them down. Then he felt a hand in his.
"It's OK, Mike. It is what it is. We never expected this to happen so let's just make the best of what we have."
It was his wife being her usual reassuring self followed by a nod from his youngest daughter to let him know that it was alright. Well, at least as alright as it could ever be.
"How long have we got, Dad?"

"Just tomorrow. That's why she'd like to see you this evening to be on the safe side."
Gaynor, as she always did, put a brave face on it. Ellie, however, was less successful.
"Let me do the washing up then I'll call her but please be ready that she might need to say goodbye this evening." At this, Ellie looked even more unhappy.
"Dad, why is life such a bummer at times?"
Ten minutes later with the washing up done, they sat on the sofa in readiness.
"OK?"

"OK."

"Mum, we're all here. Can we talk now?"

And there she was seeming, to him at least, to have been a little more delayed than previously and a little more tired. Gaynor quietly moved across to the other sofa to make room so that he and Ellie could sit either side of his mother. Ellie, he noticed, reached out and held her grandmother's hand tightly. His mum smiled, "I love you, Ellie. You know that, don't you?"

"Granny, I've only known you a couple of days but it feels like a lifetime. But it's a lifetime that I'd wanted to continue and now I know that we can't." Her face turned from smiling to tearful.

As Gaynor reached over to hold her daughter, his mother replied.

"I'm so sorry, Ellie, but I know that the end is very near now and, if I'm to go, I want it to be at my choosing. Not like last time. I hope you understand."

"It's OK, Granny. Dad explained and, yes, I do understand. It's just that it's hard…." Her voice trailed away.

"Michael" It was obvious that his mum wanted to say something that she found difficult.

"Mum, what is it?"

Her voice was very quiet and she looked worried.

"Just thinking about tomorrow and what it might be like." There was no easy answer and, much as he wanted to say what his intellect told him to, this was his mum and she was frightened; much as she must have been all those years ago. The only difference this time was that they were both aware of it.

"Don't any of the others know whether anyone has returned after the final goodbye to their loved ones?"

"It seems that no one ever does. So that final leaving is just that, final."

"And you've said your goodbyes?"

"No, but we will tomorrow before I come to you."

"Mum, I don't know what to say to make it better other than wherever you're going, we're all likely to finish up in the same place."
He hoped that she read into that "until we meet again", something that he didn't believe.
He who was so good with words was lost for them. Instead he reached out only to find that Ellie had already done so and was holding his mother's hand. He reached for the other one to find that Gaynor had moved over and was doing the same. Three of the most important women in his life doing what women have done for one another throughout the ages.

"We'll be there, Lou. You just have to ask for whatever you need and, if we can do it, we will."

"I know, Gaynor, I know. It's the not knowing that's hard. Last time the pain was so great that it was a relief to go. This time the only pain is in here."
She pointed at her heart as Gaynor took his hand and put it into his mother's. Then, as she and Ellie stepped back, he put his arms around her doing his best to comfort her.
Is she alright?
Not really, little man, but we both have to be strong. The last thing she needs is us to let her know that we're upset too. That would make it worse.
I can be strong. I was last time.
I know you were. And I know that you will be.
Remember the fun you and mum had together and the good times before I came along.
We've had good times, haven't we?
We've managed, Michael, and we will do again. So, try not to worry. I'm here.
This wasn't the time to let him know what was to happen to him tomorrow.

"Michael, Gaynor, Ellie, if you don't mind, I think I'll leave now and see you tomorrow. I'm tired and I have to do something that I'm not looking forward to. See you tomorrow. Call me. Love you all."
Then, before they could respond, she was gone and, once

181

again, they were each left with their thoughts and the knowledge that tomorrow would be the final goodbye.

The Farewell and an Unexpected Reunion

He got up to the thought of how his life, all their lives, had changed beyond measure in the last week or so. And how they would change for the worse today.

Come on, Michael. You can do this and, anyway, you've no choice. Let her go in her own way.

Is it today?

Yes, Michael, it is. Try not to worry, we've got each other.

Will you be there for me always?

Always, Michael. You must know that. We both need to be strong, just like last time. Anyway, there won't be two of us anymore. You never knew it but you grew up to be me a long time ago.

So, if you want to, let's cry together for the last time so that you can be at peace as well.

Will you hold me?

You know I will. Have I ever let you down?

The voice inside was so quiet that he could hardly hear it.

I don't think so.
And I won't now.
As he put his arm around himself and hugged tightly, he heard himself calling her name.

"Are you alright, my son."

"Yes, Mum, I am. I'm just saying goodbye to someone I've cared for for years and now we can both say goodbye."

"Little Michael?"

"Yes, little Michael. He's going with you so that you can keep each other company."

"Really, I'd like that."

"So will he."

"I'm glad you're my mum."

"And I'm glad you're my son."

"Is this it already?

"Not quite. Ellie and Gaynor are here aren't they?"

"Yes, Gaynor isn't working today and Ellie's told them that she won't be in until tomorrow. So there's no rush. Is there any pressure on you and have you talked to the others?"

She smiled, "No pressure. I'm still in control and I intend for it to stay that way. And, yes, I have talked to the others. It was sad as we've known each other for years but it was also quite calm; something that I hadn't really expected. They all send their love by the way."
He laughed, "This is like 'Truly, Madly, Deeply'"
"Pardon."

"Just a lovely film about someone who dies and ghosts and parting, Mum. It always make me cry."
She looked at the television, "Do you mind. I'd like to watch something while you have your breakfast. Is that OK?"

"Of course. 'Midwife' then Ellie and Gaynor can watch it with you.
For one last time.
It was a strange couple of hours with all of them trying to act as "normally" as possible and three knowing that, within a short space of time, they would still be here while one of them wouldn't. In an effort to ensure that his routine should continue, he went out to get his newspaper but couldn't concentrate enough to read it. The EU and the UK were still deadlocked over the Irish border deal and there were safety fears due to junior doctors being left to run A & E departments. Same old, same old. In the meantime, the elephant in the room grew larger. And something else that he really should have thought about. That's the problem with a lack of empathy, you don't always notice. Only now he did.
"You OK, Mum?"

"Just a bit frightened, my child. I know, I have no choice and I need to go but, after tomorrow, there won't be a "me" anymore. The thought of seeing you sustained me for all those years and now it won't ever again. What will happen after that? Maybe I was better off before, in limbo. Didn't you say that, very early on, you found out that journeys were better than destinations? It could be that they are. And this is worse as the journey will be on my own."

"Mum, have you forgotten what I just said? Michael will be going with you to keep you company."

"My god, I had forgotten. It'll be just like old times."
So the end is accompanied by memory loss.
He smiled, "Yes, the two of you together, just like it used

to be in the early days."

"But how?"

"Like you, I'm not entirely sure, so let's just do what seems right."

"Michael, little man, it's me."
I'm here

"Can you come out now?"
No, better in here.

"Really it's OK. There's someone here who wants to see you."
People can't see me. Safe in here.

"Come on, little man, just for a minute. Then you can go back if you want to."
Promise?

"Of course. Have I ever let you down?"
No.

"And I still won't. I just want you to see someone. Someone important."
To look after me?

"Of course. Trust me."
He felt a small hand creep round from behind him and slide into his. Then another hand so that two small arms encircled his right leg.

"See, it's OK. No one will hurt you."
They did before.

"But not this time. I promise."
He looked down to see a mop of blond curly hair (where had that gone?) above big, wary, blue eyes.

"Michael?" It was his mother's voice trembling as if she couldn't believe what she was seeing.
The child stepped out further to be swept up in his

186

mother's arms. His hands cupped her face so that their eyes were within inches of one another. And how those eyes shone.

"Mummy. Where have you been?"

"It's a long story, my child."
She reached out to the person that the child had become and hugged him.

"You, my son, are amazing. My god, how I love you."

"Love you too, Mum."
His mother then embraced Gaynor and Ellie.
She shook her head in wonder.
"You two are very special and I know that my son is in good hands."

"We'll miss you, Granny."
Ellie was crying as was her father. To one side he heard Gaynor catch her breath just like she did in Long Lost Families.
"Michael, you're going with Mummy now."

"You OK?"

"Of course. Never better."
Not quite true but it didn't matter.

"Where are we going, Mummy?"

"On a long journey, my little man."

"Can't big Mike come with us?"

"No, not this time but we'll see him again, I'm sure."

"Don't want to leave him, Mummy. He needs me."

"Yes, but look, this is Ellie and this is Gaynor and

they'll look after him now."

"I look after him better."

She smiled, "I'm sure that you do, my child, but now it's their turn."

"You sure?"

"Yes, very sure. I know them and I know how much they care."

Fortunately he had a small child's attention span,

"Where are we going?"

"On a nice journey and one that we should have taken together many years ago?"

"Why didn't we?"

"Mummy had another journey to take but now she's back to take you with her."

"When are we going?"

She looked over at her son and his family and his heart broke.

"Now's as good a time as any, my child."

"I know, Mum, I know."

He looked at Gaynor and Ellie and they nodded. Their faces not able to hide the enormity of the occasion.

"OK. I love you, Ada Louisa Hudson, and now I know you too. You don't know how good that feels."

"Oh but I do, my child, because I've got to know the person you became and I'm immensely proud of you. Never, ever forget that I lived and that you were the most important thing in my whole life. Always remember that. Always."

They were all in tears and, for a short while the rest of the world was an irrelevance. It really did cease to exist.

"Goodbye, my son, my special child and God bless you. Ellie, have a good life and be who you want to be. And don't forget the granny who came to visit and how much she loved you. And you, Gaynor, my beautiful daughter in law. Thank you for making my son happy. From what he's told me, it can't have been easy at times." She laughed. "May you have many happy years ahead of you both. And don't forget to tell Tracey and Matt and my great grandchildren that I loved them too and I'm glad to have known them."

It was then that he felt what he had been dreading for the past few days. A slipping away. Not a tugging, a pulling, but a sense of dislocation. It was as if something or, awful thought, someone was in the wrong place. That they needed, finally, to get to where they were meant to be. He also knew that there was nothing he could do to stop that happening. The power of the emotion that had brought them together and sustained them now seemed to be working in reverse. His mind flashed back to a time when Matt had been pulled from his grasp in the melee after a football match. Fortunately then, someone rescued him. This time there would be no such respite.

"It's alright, Michael, you can let me go. I'm where I need to be and I'm not afraid. I have my little man with me. It's OK, it really is. Goodbye, my child. Be happy. Think of me. Godbless. Take care." It was as if she was trying to compress as many sentiments as she could into those final few seconds. "I love you more than you could ever know." Then, in his head, he heard an old familiar refrain.

"You are my sunshine, my only sunshine.
You make me happy when skies are grey.
You'll never know, dear, how much I love you,
So please don't take my sunshine away."

And, as they watched she and Michael, she sad, he smiling, faded from view and the room was quiet. Like the grave.

For a short while, they were lost in their own thoughts until he could be strong no longer. Tears poured out from him as years of subdued grief took over. It took Gaynor and Ellie, each experiencing their own loss, some

189

minutes to comfort him. Eventually, the tears subsided and he was left with an enormous feeling of emptiness. He would never see his mother again and that thought overwhelmed him. It was then that he felt the full extent of the emotional draining that he'd experienced and he collapsed onto the sofa.

"Dad, would you like a cup of tea?"
It was Ellie, quietly getting on with what needed to be done.
He managed to say "Yes please, my love."

"Coffee, Mum."

"Please."
Minutes later, he was holding the cup with both hands as if his whole body needed the warmth, which it did. The hot drink helped but it was no substitute. Without realising it, he heard himself say "I'd like to go to the cemetery this afternoon. Do you two want to come along."

"Of course."

"With a bunch of white roses, Dad."
He didn't want to spoil things by telling his daughter that he'd recently put some on her grave. While smiling at the thought that her consideration showed that, no matter how bad she felt, he was actually one very lucky person. Now to ring Tracey and Matt to explain why he hadn't been able to ring them beforehand. And to get that headstone ordered.

Resting in Peace

Having gone to sleep following the sort of damp November evening that he disliked so much, he awoke to one of those lovely crisp mornings in which an English winter can excel. It was, in short, just the day for a visit to a very atmospheric, old cemetery. Unfortunately, none of them had had an undisturbed night's sleep so it was later than they'd planned before they got underway. Still, it was a Sunday and they had all day. Also, Nunhead was a perfect haven from life in a city over which it had perfect views; its tranquility just what they needed on that morning above all others.

The train journey, as it passed through south London, evoked the usual childhood memories. Past the flat that Aunt Ada and Uncle Bill moved into on the Neckinger Estate before the train stopped at Nunhead Station. After dropping in at the garden centre near the cemetery, they walked to the main gates and up the central avenue before turning right. Then up the short incline before the path fell away and down to the grave. The cross was still in place to mark its location as were the flowers that he's placed a few days ago. With his wife and youngest daughter on either side of him, he topped the small rise; his footsteps slowing to allow him to gather his thoughts. There his mother lay, finally at peace.

"You OK, Dad?" It was Ellie who'd noticed that he was holding back.

"Yeah, thank you, my love." This in the almost inaudible voice that was his default mode for sad occasions. "You?"

"Erhuh." Also a default mode for similar reasons.

"Gaynor?"

"Yes. Now let's go and replenish those flowers."
A few minutes later, with more of her favourite flowers decorating his mother's grave, they all stood quietly over where she lay. In peace.
"The next time we visit there should be a headstone there. Something that will show future generations where my mum is. I like that thought."
Another minute passed before Gaynor said, "Mike, I'm just going to go for a short walk so that you can have some time, well, you know. Are you coming, Ellie?"

"In a minute."
So his wife left her husband and daughter to their thoughts; as he knew that she would.
"You alright, Dad?"

"Not too bad. I think this is maybe the first step to acknowledging that she's really dead. It does feel good, though, to know for definite where she is and that I can be almost within arm's reach of her whenever I want to be."

"I'm so glad that I had the chance to get to know her. Even if she was a ghost. It's something that I'll never forget and any children that I do have will come here just as we've done."
He reached out to hold her hand.

"I love you, Ellie, and so did she."

"Ditto on both counts, Dad. Now I think you could do

with a few minutes on your own so I'm off to find mum."
He nodded. "I won't be long and I'll text you when I'm
ready."

As she walked off, he again thanked his lucky stars.

*Mum, thanks for everything. I think we probably said it all
while we were together but I just wanted to be here where you
are today. You came to me for a while and now I can come to you
whenever I want. After all, the cemetery is a lovely place to visit
in its own right. In fact, when it's my turn, I'd like some of my
ashes scattered where you are. Also, I hope you like the flowers.
Ellie insisted that we bring them. Two bunches within a week
when you've probably never had any before. Anyway, the next
step is that headstone. That should be in place early in the new
year; something plain with a simple inscription. I hope you don't
mind but, although you've always been Ada Louisa Hudson to
me, I need to put Daligan on the stone. Anyone who visits will
then know that you were Mike Daligan's mother.*

*So, now that you're at peace, I'm going to try to get on with the
rest of my life. It won't be easy but it will be with the knowledge
that I knew what you were like. So, take care, Mum. I'll see you
again sometime. Love you.*

And, with that he walked away feeling extremely sad but
with an ease about the fact that she was dead that he'd probably never had before. So she wasn't the only one who was
now resolved. As he got to the footpath, he reached into his
pocket for his mobile. The text that he sent read, "Gaynor,
where are you? I think I'm done here. Love you."

A Fitting Memorial

It was late the following Spring that he next visited the cemetery. In the meantime, ownership of the grave had been transferred from his father to himself, the necessary permissions obtained and a headstone made and erected. It was a plain white stone which bore the carving of a rose, space for additional names and a simple inscription:

In Loving Memory
of

Ada Louisa Daligan
23 December 1912 to 19 November 1947

To my mum from your son, Michael
Found you at last

That should intrigue anyone who didn't know the story and please everyone who did. He just thought that it best reflected what had happened and had a nice ring to it. Now to write that book. When it was finished, perhaps he could come here and read bits to her. He quite liked that thought. As he did when he considered that this would be where he, too, would finally rest when they would be together. And with those thoughts, he picked up his rucksack and headed for home. Still with a heavy heart but, somehow, a lighter step. No doubt that there would be sadness ahead but, for now, he felt that the jigsaw was complete. The child and his mother were together again and the adult, well, he could get on with the rest of his life without the large hole that had been part of it for so long. Rest in Peace, Mum.

Printed in Great Britain
by Amazon